THE
RULES
OF
MANAGEMENT

THE
RULES
OF
MANAGEMENT

A definitive code for
managerial success

RICHARD TEMPLAR

PEARSON

Harlow, England • London • New York • Boston • San Francisco • Toronto • Sydney
Auckland • Singapore • Hong Kong • Tokyo • Seoul • Taipei • New Delhi
Cape Town • São Paulo • Mexico City • Madrid • Amsterdam • Munich • Paris • Milan

PEARSON EDUCATION LIMITED
Edinburgh Gate
Harlow CM20 2JE
Tel: +44 (0)1279 623623
Web: www.pearson.com/uk

First published 2005 (print and electronic)
Second edition published 2011 (print and electronic)
Third edition published 2013 (print and electronic)
This edition published 2015 (print and electronic)

© Richard Templar 2005 (print and electronic)
© Richard Templar and Pearson Education Limited 2011, 2013 (print and electronic)
© Richard Templar 2015 (print and electronic)

The right of Richard Templar to be identified as author of this work has been asserted by him in accordance with the Copyright, Designs and Patents Act 1988.

Pearson Education is not responsible for the content of third-party internet sites.

ISBN: 978-1-292-08800-6 (print)
      978-1-292-08802-0 (PDF)
      978-1-292-08803-7 (ePub)
      978-1-292-08801-3 (eText)

British Library Cataloguing-in-Publication Data
A catalogue record for the print edition is available from the British Library

Library of Congress Cataloging-in-Publication Data
A catalog record for the print edition is available from the Library of Congress

10 9 8 7 6 5 4 3 2 1
19 18 17 16 15

Cover design by Nick Redeyoff

Print edition typeset in 10.5/12pt ITC Berkeley Oldstyle Std by 71
Print edition printed and bound in Great Britain by Clays Ltd, Bungay, Suffolk

NOTE THAT ANY PAGE CROSS REFERENCES REFER TO THE PRINT EDITION

Contents

Managing yourself 78

The Rules for entrepreneurs 220

Introduction

Strange thing, management. It's something few of us set out in life to do, yet most of us find ourselves doing at some point.

> *Careers adviser:* What would you like to do when you leave school?

> *16-year-old:* I want to be a manager.

Did this happen to you? No, me neither. But here you are anyway.

As a manager you are expected to be a lot of things. A tower of strength, a leader and innovator, a magician (conjuring up pay rises, resources and extra staff at the drop of a hat), a kindly uncle/aunt, a shoulder to cry on, a dynamic motivator, a stern but fair judge, a diplomat, a politician, a financial wizard (no, this is quite different from being a magician), a protector, a saviour and a saint.

You are responsible for a whole gang of people that you probably didn't pick, may not like, might have nothing in common with and who perhaps won't like you much. You have to coax out of them a decent day's work. You are also responsible for their physical, emotional and mental safety and care. You have to make sure they don't hurt themselves – or each other. You have to ensure they can carry out their jobs according to whatever legislation your industry warrants. You have to know your rights, their rights, the company's rights, the union's rights.

And on top of all this, you're expected to do your job as well.

Oh yes, and you have to remain cool and calm – you can't shout, throw things or have favourites. This management business is a tall order . . .

You are responsible for looking after and getting the best out of a team. This team may behave at times like small children – and you can't smack them* (or possibly even sack them). At other times they will behave like petulant teenagers – sleeping in late, not turning up, refusing to do any real work if they do turn up, sloping off early, that sort of thing.

Like you, I've managed teams (in my case, of up to 100 people at a time). People whose names I was expected to know, and all their little foibles – ah, Heather can't work late on a Tuesday because her daughter has to be collected from play group; Trevor is colour blind so we can't use him at the trade show; Mandy sulks if left to answer the phones at lunchtime and loses us customers; Chris is great in a team but can't motivate herself to do anything solo; Ray drinks and shouldn't be allowed to drive himself anywhere.

As a manager, you are also expected to be a buffer zone between higher management and your staff. Nonsense may come down from on high but you have to (a) sell it to your team, (b) not groan loudly or laugh, and (c) get your team to work with it even if it is nonsense.

You also have to justify the 'no pay rises this year' mentality even if it has just completely demotivated your team. You will have to keep secret any knowledge you have of takeovers, mergers, acquisitions, secret deals, senior management buyouts and the like, despite the fact that rumours are flying and you are being constantly asked questions by your team.

You are responsible not only for people but also for budgets, discipline, communications, efficiency, legal matters, union matters, health and safety matters, personnel matters, pensions, sick pay, maternity leave, paternity leave, holidays, time off, time out, time sheets, whip rounds and leaving presents, rotas, industry standards, fire drills, first aid, fresh air, heating, plumbing,

---

* Yes, yes, I know you can't smack children either. I was just making a point. Please don't write in.

parking spaces, lighting, stationery, resources, and teas and coffees. And that's not to mention the small matter of customers.

And you will have to fight with other departments, other teams, clients, senior bosses, senior management, the board, shareholders and the accounts department (unless of course you are the manager of the accounts department).

You are also expected to set standards. This means you are going to have to be an on-time, upfront, smartly dressed, hard-working, industrious, late-staying, early-rising, detached, responsible, caring, knowledgeable, above-reproach juggler. Tall order.

You also need to accept that as a manager you may be ridiculed – think *The Office* – derided as a manipulative obstructionist pen pusher – think *Yes Minister* – and possibly even judged by your staff, shareholders and/or the public to be ineffective and even superfluous to the carrying out of the actual job in hand.*

And all you wanted to do was your job . . . Luckily there are a few hints and tips that will have you sailing through it looking cool, gaining points and coming up smelling of roses. These are the Rules of management – the unwritten, unspoken, unacknowledged Rules. Keep them to yourself if you want to stay one step ahead of the game.

Management is an art and a science. There are textbooks of thousands of pages devoted to how to do it. There are countless training courses (you've probably been on a few). However, what no textbook contains and no training course includes are

---

* If this all makes you feel a bit bleak about being a manager – don't be. Managers are the stuff that runs the world. We get to lead, to inspire, to motivate, to guide, to shape the future. We get to make a difference to the business and to people's lives. We get to make a real and positive contribution to the state of the world. We get not only to be part of the solution but to provide the solution itself. We are the sheriff and the marshal and the ranger all rolled into one. We are the engine and the captain. It's a great role and we should relish it – it's just not always an easy role . . .

the various 'unwritten' rules that make you a good, effective and decent manager – the Rules of management. Whether you are responsible for only one or two people or thousands – it doesn't matter. The Rules are the same.

You won't find anything here you probably didn't already know. Or if you didn't know it, then you will read it and say, 'But that's really bleeding obvious'. Yes, it is all really bleeding obvious, if you think hard enough about it. But in the fast-paced, frantic, just-about-coping kind of life we lead, you may not have thought about it lately. And what isn't so obvious is whether or not you do it.

I've arranged these Rules for you into two sections:

- managing your team
- managing yourself.

I think that should be fairly simple. The Rules aren't arranged in any particular order of importance – the first ones aren't more important than later ones or vice versa. Read them all and then start to put them into practice, adopting the ones that seem easiest to you first. A lot of them will flow together so that you can begin to carry them out simultaneously, unconsciously. Soon we'll have you looking cool and relaxed, confident and assertive, in charge, in control, on top of things and managing marvellously. Not bad considering it wasn't too long ago you were shoulder to the wheel, nose to the grindstone, ear to the ground and back to the wall. Well done you.

Before we begin, it might be worth taking a moment or two to determine what exactly we all mean by 'management'. And that isn't as easy as it sounds. For my money we are all managers – parents, the self-employed, the entrepreneur, the employed, even the ones who inherited wealth. We all have to 'manage'. It might only be ourselves, but we still have to cope, to make the best use of the resources available, motivate, plan, process, facilitate, monitor, measure success, set standards, budget, execute and work. It's just that some of us have to do all that with bigger teams. But the fundamental stuff doesn't change.

The Harvard Business School defines a manager as someone who 'gets results through other people'. The great management consultant Peter Drucker says a manager is 'someone who has the responsibility to plan, execute and monitor'; while the Australian Institute of Management's definition of a manager is a person who 'plans, leads, organizes, delegates, controls, evaluates and budgets in order to achieve an outcome'. I can go along with that.

It can get very wordy and complex:

> A Manager is an employee who forms part of the organization's management team and is accountable for exercising delegated authority over human, financial, and material management to accomplish the objectives of the organization. Managers are responsible for managing human resources, communicating, practising and promoting the corporate values, ethics and culture of the organization, and for leading and managing change within the organization. (The Leadership Network, California)

Fine, whatever. We are all managers in whatever form or shape we think and we all have to get on with the job of managing. Anything that makes our life simpler is a bonus. Here are the simple Rules of management. They aren't devious or underhand. Actually they are all pretty obvious. But if you think about each carefully and implement each without fail, you'll be amazed what a difference it will make to your work and your life.

You may *know* everything in this book, but do you *do* it? This book will help motivate you into doing what you already know.

If you have any comments or indeed Rules of your own to pass on, you can post your very own on my Facebook page at www.facebook.com/richardtemplar

Richard Templar

MANAGING YOUR TEAM

We all have to work with people. These may be loosely known as a team or a department or a squad or a crew – even a posse. It doesn't matter. The mistake a lot of managers make is to think they are managing people. They think that people are their tools, their stock-in-trade. Make the people successful and you have the successful manager – or so the theory goes.

But unfortunately this is a myth and we need to see that the real role of the manager is to manage processes rather than people. People can manage themselves if you let them. What you need to be concentrating on is the real job of management – the strategy. The team is merely a means to fulfilling that end. If all your people could be replaced by machines – and how many of us haven't prayed that this might happen? – we would still have to have a strategy, still have to be managing the process.

Of course we, as managers, have to work with real flesh-and-blood people and we have to know what motivates them, how they think and feel, why they come to work, why they give of their best (or their worst), what they are afraid of, what they hope for and dream of. We shall have to encourage them, coach them, give them the resources to do their job and manage themselves, oversee their processes and set their strategy for them. We will worry about them, look out for them, be on their side and support them. But we won't manage them. We will let them manage themselves and we shall concentrate on our real role as a manager.

RULE 1

Get them emotionally involved

You manage people. People who are paid to do a job. But if it is 'just a job' to them, you'll never get their best. If they come to work looking to clock in and clock off and do as little as they can get away with in-between, then you're doomed to failure, my friend. On the other hand, if they come to work looking to enjoy themselves, looking to be stretched, challenged, inspired and to get involved, then you are in with a big chance of getting the very best out of them. Trouble is, the jump from drudge to super team is entirely down to you. It is *you* that has to inspire them, lead them, motivate them, challenge them, get them emotionally involved.

That's OK. You like a challenge yourself, don't you? The good news is that getting a team emotionally involved is easy. All you have to do is make them care about what they are doing. And that's easy too. You have to get them to see the relevance of what they are doing, how it makes an impact on people's lives, how they provide for the needs of other human beings, how they can reach out and touch people by what they do at work. Get them convinced – because it is true of course – that what they do makes a difference, that it contributes to society in some way rather than just lines the owner's or shareholders' pockets, or ensures that the chief executive gets a big fat pay cheque.

And yes, I know it's easier to show how they contribute if you manage nurses rather than an advertising sales team, but if you think about it, then you can find value in any role and instil pride in those who do whatever job it is. Prove it? OK. Well, those who sell advertising space are helping other companies, some of which may be very small, reach their markets. They are alerting potential customers to things they may have wanted for a long time and may really need. They are keeping the newspaper or magazine afloat as it relies on ad sales income, and that magazine or newspaper delivers information and/or gives pleasure to the people who buy it (otherwise they wouldn't, would they?).

Get them to care because that's an easy thing to do. Look, this is a given. Everyone deep down wants to be valued and to be useful. The cynics will say this is nonsense, but it is true, deep down true. All you have to do is reach down far enough and you will find care, feeling, concern, responsibility and involvement. Drag all that stuff up and they'll follow you forever and not even realize why.

Oh, just make sure that you've convinced yourself first before you try this out on your team. Do you believe that what you do makes a positive difference? If you're not sure, reach down, deep down, and find a way of caring . . .

> GET THEM CONVINCED –
> BECAUSE IT IS TRUE OF
> COURSE – THAT WHAT THEY
> DO MAKES A DIFFERENCE

RULE 2

Know what a team is and how it works

So what is a team and how does it operate? If we are going to be successful managers we have to know the answers to these questions.

A team isn't a collection of people. It is an organization with its own dynamics, qualities and conventions. Without knowing these things you will flounder. Knowing them, you can work your team to achieve greatness.

In every team there are a variety of people all pushing and shoving in different directions and with unequal force. Some shove louder, if you know what I mean. Others are happy to push from the back. Others don't appear to be doing anything, but you'll need them for ideas.

If you haven't looked at team dynamics before, I urge you to read Meredith Belbin's *Management Teams: Why they succeed or fail.** (If you have, pass right on to the next Rule.) This is designed for managers concerned with achieving results by getting the best from their key people. I'll paraphrase what he says, but I do urge you to practise what he preaches.

Belbin says that there are nine team roles – and we all carry out one or more functions of these team roles. Yes, it is fun to identify our own, but it is much more useful to identify your team's and then work with that information.

The nine team roles are the Plant (that's the ideas person), the Resource Investigator, the Co-ordinator, the Shaper, the Monitor

---

* *Management Teams: Why they succeed or fail* by R. Meredith Belbin (Butterworth-Heinemann, 3rd edition, 2010).

Evaluator, the Team Worker, the Implementer, the Completer and the Specialist. If you want to know more, you'll have to read the book.

Now you know who you might have in your team. So what exactly is a team and how are you going to make yours more effective? Again, read Belbin and also come to understand a team is a group where all the members focus on a collective target. A team doesn't pull together well when each individual member focuses on their own target – be that just getting to the end of the day, their own personal progress, how to stitch up the boss (that's you, by the way), use work as a social club, etc.

You'll know you have a team when you hear 'we' and 'us' more often than 'I' and 'me'.

You'll know you have a team when difficult decisions become easy – because someone says, 'It's OK, we're all in this together'.

You'll know you have a team when the team tells you it is a team.

> ## A TEAM DOESN'T PULL TOGETHER WELL WHEN EACH INDIVIDUAL MEMBER FOCUSES ON THEIR OWN TARGET

RULE 3

Set realistic targets – no, really realistic

When I was doing the research for this book, someone said that setting realistic targets was unrealistic and that all targets should be 'stretching' ones because that would impress the board. Now, can you see the problem here? Yep, we're not talking here about motivating a team, getting a job done, creating an atmosphere of success and creativity. No, we're talking about impressing the board. Now on paper that might be a smart thing to do if your board is made up of monkeys, but I bet it isn't. I bet it's made up of pretty shrewd cookies who would see through a manoeuvre like that in a nanosecond.

When I say realistic, I don't say lower or easy-to-achieve targets. I say realistic. That might mean taxing. It might mean a struggle. It might mean your team has to redouble its efforts, work harder, longer, brighter. But Rule 3 says realistic and that means achievable, within your grasp. And yes, you might have to stretch a bit.

Realistic means you know what your team is capable of and what is expected of it by your bosses. Somehow you will have to marry the two to keep both sides happy. You can't pressurize your team out of existence, nor can you let your bosses think you're slacking.

If your bosses insist on setting targets that aren't realistic, you must feed that back to them. Don't argue or procrastinate; feed it back to them. Ask how they think the targets could be achieved. Say they are unrealistic. Be very well prepared, make your case that the targets are unrealistic and ask again how they think they could be achieved. Suggest a realistic target of your own, well supported by facts and figures. Keep feeding the problem back to your bosses and asking for clarification. Sooner or later they must set a more realistic target or order you to achieve the impossible. Either way, you are absolved of the problem. If they set you

8 THE RULES OF MANAGEMENT

realistic targets, then all you need to do is meet those targets (you know you can do this). If they order you to fulfil unrealistic ones, you are also in the clear; when you fail to achieve the unachievable you will be able to explain that at the time you did register your protest and bring your case back to them.

> # KEEP FEEDING THE PROBLEM BACK TO YOUR BOSSES

RULE 4

Hold effective meetings . . .

We've all been to them – the meetings that drag on, people who ramble, agendas written on the back of an envelope or spur of the moment, any-other-business surprises, lack of information, insufficient notice.

As a manager you will have to hold meetings. Make them effective. Decide in advance what the objective of the meeting is and make sure you meet that objective.

Basically, meetings have only four purposes:

- to create and fuse a team
- to impart information
- to brainstorm ideas (and make decisions)
- to collect information (and make decisions).

Some meetings might well take in one or more of these, but you should still be aware of that and add it into your objective. If your meeting is to impart information, then do it and get the hell out. If it's a discussion about that information you want, then that's a different type of meeting and as such should have different objectives.

Be aware that some meetings are there to help your team meet each other, bond, socialize together, find out about each other and see you in your true role as team leader.

If you want your meetings to be effective, then remain firmly in control – no wishy-washy democracies here. You are the manager and you are in charge – end of story. To be effective you shouldn't allow anyone to reminisce, ramble, rabbit on, refuse to shut up or relax. Keep 'em moving fast and get them out of the door as soon as you can.

DECIDE IN ADVANCE WHAT
THE OBJECTIVE OF THE
MEETING IS AND MAKE SURE
YOU MEET THAT OBJECTIVE

RULE 5

... No, really effective

Right, now you're sure this meeting is necessary, and what it's for, let's keep it as brief and effective as possible.

Hold all meetings at the end of the day rather than at the beginning. Everyone's anxious to be off home and it keeps meetings shorter; at the beginning of the day everyone has ages to digress and chat. Unless of course it is a bonding meeting; you can cheerfully hold them at the beginning of business.

See how many meetings you could hold by e-mail, phone, one-to-one (cut out everyone who isn't absolutely essential).

Start all meetings on time. Never wait for anyone. Never go back over stuff for latecomers. If they've missed something vital they can get it from others after the meeting and it'll learn 'em to be on time next time.* Useful tip – never schedule meetings to begin exactly on the hour, always say 3.10 rather than 3 o'clock. You'll find people will always be more punctual if you set an 'odd' time. Try 3.35 if you want to be really wacky.

Schedule the meeting far enough in advance – but not too far – so that no one can say they had something else on. Confirm the day before with everyone to make sure they have remembered and can make it.

---

* The Toad, having finished his breakfast, picked up a stout stick and swung it vigorously, belabouring imaginary animals. 'I'll learn 'em to steal my house!' he cried. 'I'll learn 'em, I'll learn 'em!' 'Don't say "learn 'em," Toad,' said the Rat, greatly shocked. 'It's not good English.' 'What are you always nagging at Toad for?' inquired the Badger, rather peevishly. 'What's the matter with his English? It's the same what I use myself, and if it's good enough for me, it ought to be good enough for you!' 'I'm very sorry,' said the Rat humbly. 'Only I THINK it ought to be "teach 'em", not "learn 'em."' 'But we don't WANT to teach 'em,' replied the Badger. 'We want to LEARN 'em – learn 'em, learn 'em! And what's more, we're going to DO it, too!' (*The Wind in the Willows* by Kenneth Grahame).

You decide who keeps the minutes – and make sure they do, and to your liking. You don't have to be bossy or aggressive about this, just firm, friendly and utterly in control.

Make sure every point on the agenda ends up with an action plan – no action plan means it was just a chat. Or make a decision of course.

You don't do 'any other business' – ever. If it's important it should be on the agenda. If it isn't, then it shouldn't be there at all. 'Any other business' is invariably someone trying to get something over on someone else. Don't allow it – ever.

If meetings are getting too big – more than six people – start to subdivide them into committees and get your committees to report back.

And most important of all – engrave this one on your heart – all meetings must have a definite purpose. At the end of the meeting you must be able to say whether or not you met that purpose. Oh yes, and hold all meetings on uncomfortable chairs (or standing, à la *West Wing*) – that speeds things up considerably.

START ALL MEETINGS ON TIME. NEVER WAIT FOR ANYONE

RULE 6

Make meetings fun

I guess that when you were working your way up to your illustrious position of today you had to sit through many interminable meetings, all boring, all stupifyingly dull. Well, the pattern has to be broken somewhere and I'm relying on you to break it. The old way of doing meetings has to stop and you're the very person to do the stopping.

So let's make 'em fun. Now, before we go on, I remember a tip I read somewhere. Basically you were supposed to give out five coins to each meeting member and when they wanted to speak they had to spend a penny. Once they had used up their coins they were done and dusted and couldn't say anything more. It was supposed to make people really cautious about speaking and reluctant to spend all their coins on trivia. Fun? Maybe. But it would also get you quite a reputation as a prat and/or an ineffectual meeting leader. As would other suggestions such as:

- fancy dress
- food and/or drink (unless it's lunchtime, in which case that's functional not fun; or if you take your team out to a restaurant or down the pub, and then it's not a meeting, it's a bonding session – or a thank you of course: see Rule 20)
- games, quizzes or contests of any sort
- having small surprises such as chocolates strapped under the chairs
- a talking stick (don't ask – a New Age Californian thing)
- blindfolds
- letting the most junior member chair the meeting.

All of these head towards farce, ruin and idiocy. Don't go there.

So how can you fun things up without looking like David Brent? Well, for a start, fun doesn't have to mean silly or stupid or unfunny.

Fun means not being stuffy, allowing people to be themselves and to bring their own contribution. Fun means allowing people to share things that have made them laugh without being frowned on. Fun is about letting people tell stories or anecdotes that lighten the mood (just know when to say, 'Right, back to business'). Fun means being flexible enough to allow other suggestions as to where and how you all meet. Perhaps your organization has a great boardroom – could you meet there? Or outside if the weather is good.

The confident manager – that's you – can be flexible because they are relaxed and cool and confident. The stuffy manager is frightened because they feel insecure and seek a rigid approach to prop up their lack of self-confidence.

> # THE OLD WAY OF DOING MEETINGS HAS TO STOP AND YOU'RE THE VERY PERSON TO DO THE STOPPING

Make your team better than you

A really good manager – yep, that's you again – knows that when their team takes wing and soars, they too will soar. Getting your team to soar takes courage, grit, determination and an overwhelming passion.

You have to make members of your team better than you, which means trusting them, getting them the best resources, training them to take over from you, trusting them not to stab you in the back when it's time to take over from you and being confident enough in your own abilities not to be jealous of them when they do take off. Tall order.

It takes quite some manager to carry this one out. You have to be pretty relaxed and secure in your own position. Encouraging your team to bring it on takes guts, quite frankly.

Let's take a look at your team. Who've you got there? Which ones will one day fill your shoes? What can you share with them to bring them on?

Shoe-fillers are the ones you want to cultivate and grow. They are the bright ones, the keen ones, the eager beavers. I once had a young assistant who was so sharp he scared me. But when I did move on up, he filled my shoes. And he came with me over several moves, always one step behind. Now the crazy thing was he was better than me in lots of ways but he never chanced his arm and overtook me. It could have been out of respect but I doubt it – the industry I worked in was a little cut-throat to say the least. No, it was habit.

Once you've built a good team it gets in the habit of having you as the manager and then it feels comfortable with that and doesn't mutiny or overtake you. Teams only do that when they feel resentful or mistrusted. So bring 'em on and train 'em up and make 'em better.

> ONCE YOU'VE BUILT A
> GOOD TEAM IT GETS IN
> THE HABIT OF HAVING
> YOU AS THE MANAGER

RULE 8

Know your own importance

You are the most important person in your team, and you'd better know it. No, not because you're a better person or more experienced or more valuable or anything to get big-headed about. You're the most important person because everyone else will take their lead from you. You set the bar.

If you play dirty, backstab, worry that your team members are better than you, spy on them, try to stop them outshining you, or are unethical, disrespectful, or anything else of the sort, then you're not going to excel as a manager, and your team will be so busy checking over their shoulders that they won't perform, and your department won't shine.

Maybe you don't get involved in all that nasty stuff? Good, pleased to hear it. But it won't help much either if you whinge, complain about directors or customers, take a negative view, resist change, talk about how much you're looking forward to Friday afternoon, always take the easy option, avoid hard work – your team will copy all those things instead.

Listen, if you don't set the standard, raise the tone, be the person you want your team to be, then you won't be a truly great manager. Your team is like a flock of birds or sheep or, well, anything that comes in a flock.* Where one goes, they all go. And you're the one they all follow. If you shine, everyone shines. If you fail, everyone fails. Because of you. Scary, huh?

But it's OK. Because you can be that brilliant manager they need to lead them. And when you are, they'll be a brilliant team full of brilliant people. Not only will you succeed personally, but you'll

---

* Except maybe wallpaper.

bring success to everyone around you. You'll approach every task with enthusiasm backed up by solid analysis and common-sense strategies. You'll treat people around you fairly, and encourage others, and deliver better than you promised, and create a positive atmosphere, and so will everyone around you. Because of you.

> # IF YOU DON'T SET THE STANDARD, RAISE THE TONE, BE THE PERSON YOU WANT YOUR TEAM TO BE, THEN YOU WON'T BE A TRULY GREAT MANAGER

RULE 9

Set your boundaries

You have to, right from day one, be totally on top of the discipline issue. Remember earlier we talked about how looking after your team can be a bit like being a parent? Well, as a parent you pretty well have to set boundaries and practise zero tolerance to survive. Give 'em an inch and they'll take the whole rope. If you are seen to be 'soft' they'll take advantage. The good thing with clear boundaries and zero tolerance is you have a finite line – a yardstick by which you can judge everything. All you have to do is ask, 'Is this a breach of the rules?' If it is, stop it. If you do allow it, where do you stop?

Say one of your clear boundaries is timekeeping (it might be dress or customer care or whatever, but just say it's timekeeping). If one minute late is fine, what about two? If two is fine, what about three? And so on until people are wandering in at whatever time they feel like. But if you don't allow it, then that's the end of the story. You don't have to think about that particular issue any more. Whereas if you do allow infringements, small breaches, you are forever having to consider, 'Is this a step too far?' 'Can I wrest control back?' 'How far am I prepared to go?'

This doesn't mean you need to have hundreds of rules and be ridiculously inflexible. It means that you need to decide on your few key boundaries that are important to you and to the team and the business. Make them clear. And make them firm.

Remember you are dealing with a team – I will stress this again and again throughout this book – and not an individual. You might feel that for each and any person an exception can be made, but you aren't dealing with individuals – you are dealing with a team. If you are seen to be soft on one individual, then you must be soft on all. If you allow one to wander in late, then all must be allowed to wander in late. If one person can get away with breaking the rules, then all must be allowed.

The good manager is firm on inappropriate behaviour because this sends out a clear message to all the team – the message that you are a good, firm, in-control sort of manager who sets more store by what the team can achieve collectively than by being thought of as an easy-going, laid-back, nice person. Yes, individually some of the team may rate you as pretty cool if you let them get away with murder, but the team will collectively rubbish you.

> THE GOOD THING WITH ZERO TOLERANCE IS YOU HAVE A FINITE LINE – A YARDSTICK BY WHICH YOU CAN JUDGE EVERYTHING

Be ready to prune

OK, so say you've got an orchestra and you get them to play. You listen. Something wrong somewhere. Yep, that flute player is out of tune, off key and playing from a different hymn sheet. Now you have three choices:

- put up with it

- change it

- end it.

Let's have a little look at these three because, as in all things – from relationships, to life, to work, to being a parent – these three choices are the same every single time.

So, you're going to put up with it. This makes your entire orchestra sound flat, out of tune and ill-fitted to do its job properly – that of supplying sweet music to the masses. Your listening public (your objective) will not listen and will accuse you, the orchestra leader, of being a nincompoop* – and they would be right.

OK, so you're going to try to change it. Flute player X gets some retraining. They get sent on a remedial flute course – residential of course. They come back with the right hymn sheet but have decided to switch to the bassoon as they were feeling creatively hemmed in by the flute. Problem sorted. Well done for tackling it.

However, what if their report says they are tone deaf and should never have been in the orchestra in the first place and should have taken up a career sounding the fire alarm somewhere? What you can't do is then embark on another course of action where you give them the triangle to play but they mess that up too and by now the rest of the orchestra has lost confidence in you and is beginning to mutiny.

---

* They don't of course use this word, but I'm not allowed to use the word they really would use.

Time for the third course. You make them redundant. It is swift and kind. They can then go on to become a champion alarm ringer somewhere, somewhere else that is, and your orchestra recognizes you as decisive, knowing what you want, objective (you put the needs of the many before the bad playing of one) and utterly in charge. Have an extra brownie point.

Always be ready to prune dead wood, straggly growth, lousy flute players (and any other team players who don't cut the mustard).

> # NOW YOU HAVE THREE CHOICES: PUT UP WITH IT, CHANGE IT, END IT

Offload as much as you can – or dare

The good manager, and that is you from now on, knows that they manage events, processes, situations, strategies but never people. Look, let's imagine you have a big garden and decide to employ a gardener. Do you manage the gardener? No. They manage themselves quite nicely, thank you. Your job is to manage the garden. You'll decide what to plant and when and where. The gardener, like a spade or a wheelbarrow, becomes a tool in that garden and a tool you can use to manage your garden effectively. But you don't manage the gardener. They manage themselves. You tell them what you want done and they get on with it. You delegate and they dig and delve and plant and prune and tend and weed. The plants actually manage themselves as well; neither you nor the gardener actually grows anything – you both manage. The gardener is your useful assistant, your tool to getting stuff done.

Now it makes sense to give the gardener as much to do with the decision-making process as possible to free you up for long-term strategy, seeing the big picture, seasonal planning and perusing seed catalogues while sitting in the shade sipping a cooling Pimm's.

There is no point standing over the gardener while they mow lawns, weed beds, prune trees and the like. It is better to give them the job to do and then let them get on with it. Once they have finished you can check their work and make sure it is up to scratch. And then you probably won't need to do that again – don't keep checking.

And that basically is the secret of good management. Give 'em a job to do and let them get on with it. Check once or twice to make sure they've done it the way you want it done and then next time just let them get on with it. Increasingly give them more and more to do and stand back more and more from the people processes and concentrate instead on the planning processes. Build your team and then trust them to get on with it. Sometimes this will backfire and people will play up, skive off, do things badly – and hey, that'll be entirely your fault because you are the manager and it's your team. No, that's serious, it is entirely down to you. Read on and we'll find ways to make sure it doesn't happen – well, not too often anyway.

> # BUILD YOUR TEAM AND THEN TRUST THEM TO GET ON WITH IT

RULE 12

Let them make mistakes

There is an old Chinese saying that goes something like this: 'Tell me and I'll remember for an hour; show me and I'll remember for a day; but let me do it and I'll remember for ever.' Fair enough. And if you are going to let people do it then they are going to do it badly at first. They are going to make mistakes. And you are going to let them.

If you are a parent you know the agonizing thing you go through with a 2-year-old who insists they can pour their own drink – and then proceeds to spill most of it on the table. You stand by with a cloth behind your back because you know that:

- they are going to spill it
- it is you who is going to have to mop it up
- the spilling process is important and you have to let them do it and they will progress to not spilling but only once they have got the spilling out of the way first.

> TELL ME AND I'LL REMEMBER
> FOR AN HOUR; SHOW ME
> AND I'LL REMEMBER FOR A
> DAY; BUT LET ME DO IT AND
> I'LL REMEMBER FOR EVER

As a parent you do that wonderful hovering thing, ready to grab the juice if it is going to spill too much, or grab the cup if it is going over, or even grab the child if they are going to fall off the chair due to such intense concentration.

I'm not saying members of your team are like small children – well, I am actually but don't tell them – but it is imperative you learn to let them do the spilling if they are to progress. Make sure you have your cloth behind your back ready to mop up after them.

And after each spillage you don't tell them off. Instead you offer praise – 'Well done, brilliant job, incredible progress.' Try not to let them see the cloth or the mopping up.

RULE 13

Accept their limitations

As we saw earlier, effectively fusing a team together means you need several different parts – or team members. Now some of us are good at certain things and others not so. If we were all the same we wouldn't be able to work as a team – we would all be leaders or all followers and you need a combination, not either/or.

So if some members of your team aren't leaders – or followers – you have to accept that. If some are good at figure work and others not, you have to accept that. If some are good at working unsupervised and others not, you have to accept that.

And to be able to accept these things you have to know your staff pretty well. You have to know their strengths and weaknesses, good points and bad. If you don't – and I'm sure this doesn't apply to you – you will be forever trying to shove round pegs into square holes and vice versa.

You have to accept that not everyone is going to be as bright, as determined, as ambitious, as clever or as motivated as you are – praise indeed from me, but see the next Rule. Some of your team are quite possibly going to be brain dead from the feet up and you might need to practise Rule 10 before Rule 13 if there simply is no hope. But don't act in haste. You might not need a team of geniuses (in fact if you hire people far too smart for a job, they will just leave, fast).

Suppose your team contains machine operators or admin assistants. Now you don't need these good people to have Einstein brains nor to be really on the ball when it comes to brainstorming. But you do need them to be able to sit in an arse-numbing position for hours at a time concentrating on a bit of work that would drive you or me batty. Just don't go expecting them to take creative wing and soar away with new ideas, new innovations or new technologies. You have to accept their limitations, and love them for them because these limitations are their parameters by which you can get the very best out of them – their best of course. And while you're at it, have a quick check of your own limitations. What's that? You haven't got any? Come on.

> # IF WE WERE ALL THE SAME WE WOULDN'T BE ABLE TO WORK AS A TEAM – WE WOULD ALL BE LEADERS OR ALL FOLLOWERS

RULE 14

Encourage people

If you don't let people know you're pleased with them, they'll wilt. People come to work for a whole raft of reasons – most, nothing to do with the money despite what they'll tell you – and right there at the top of their unwritten, unspoken, undeclared list will be 'Praise from the boss'. That's you by the way, the boss.

They might call it 'recognition' or 'acknowledgement' or 'feeling I've done well' – but how do they know? They know because you tell them.

Now you can praise them retroactively, so to speak – wait until they've done good and then tell them they've done good – or you can encourage them in advance – active praise. Tell them they're going to do good before they've done it. Why? Because the chances of them doing good are that much greater if you have praised them in advance. They won't want to let you down, or themselves.

Being a manager is a minimalist's dream. You want to build a great team and you want to do it with the smallest output of resources. Praise is free. It is instantly replaceable, doesn't wear out, is invariably 100 per cent effective, is incredibly simple to do and takes no time at all.

So why don't more managers do it? Because it takes self-assurance. You have to be feeling pretty good about yourself to be able to dish out praise well in advance. If you doubt yourself, you'll doubt them. If you doubt them, you'll not praise them because you'll be sure they are going to screw up.

It takes nothing except courage to say, 'Come on, you can do it. You'll be fine'. The more responsibility you give people, the more you trust them, the more you praise them, the more you encourage them, the more they'll give you in return. Praise costs nothing and brings in loads. Encouragement should be a given.

Encourage an atmosphere where everyone encourages everyone else – 'You can do it' should be heard every day all around you. If you're not saying it, chances are your team isn't either. Encourage the good ones to give the less good ones a hand up. In any good team an air of fostering help should be actively encouraged and praised when it happens. We're all in this together and we sink or swim together.

> # TELL THEM THEY'RE GOING TO DO GOOD BEFORE THEY'VE DONE IT

RULE 15

Be very, very good at finding the right people

You have to be good at finding the right people to fill the right jobs – and then leave them to get on with it. OK, I know this is one rule that requires a certain intuitive touch but I'm sure you know the sort of manager I'm talking about. They seem to surround themselves with capable, competent people and then they just seem to sit back and watch them go for goal. You can do that too. It is a special talent but one you can cultivate. I guess the skill is in both picking the right people *and* letting go – leaving them alone to get on with it. You have to have lots of trust to do that; trust in their ability and trust in your own as well.

You have to have a very clear idea of *who* you are looking for to fill a job as much as *what* you are looking for. For instance, you might need a senior account manager – that is *what* you are looking for. But *who*? Team player? Good all-rounder? Someone able to make decisions on the run? Someone who can plan ahead? Someone who understands your industry's quirks? Someone who speaks fluent spreadsheets? Someone who can work with an overexcitable union?

I'm sure you get the idea. If you have a clear picture of *who* you need as well as *what* you need, you make the transition to being a manager who seems to have an uncanny knack of finding the right people. It's not a knack, of course, but planning, vision, logic and hard work.

I once made the mistake of being totally seduced by a manager's credentials – I was a general manager seeking to employ a manager – and failing to look hard enough at *who* he was rather than *what* he was. Yes, he had the credentials and was very good at his job. But he wasn't a team player and saw everything as a competition, mainly between him and the other managers. Fine in itself, but it didn't work for me or the other managers, who all wanted to pull together. This was one case where I was not good at finding the right person. I had found the wrong person and it took a lot to extricate myself. I had only myself to blame because I hadn't thought sufficiently about who I wanted.

If you're not good at this, or think you could improve, invite somebody you respect to sit in on interviews with you to give you another perspective. Find a mentor or coach to help you work out who you really need.

> **YOU HAVE TO BE GOOD AT FINDING THE RIGHT PEOPLE TO FILL THE RIGHT JOBS – AND THEN LEAVE THEM TO GET ON WITH IT**

RULE 16

Hire raw talent

Do you know how many publishers turned down the first *Harry Potter* book? I've heard several numbers quoted, but the answer is at least eight, whoever you ask. And what does that say about Barry Cunningham, the publisher who finally signed up the author? To just about everyone it says he was a whole lot smarter than all the guys who turned the book down.

Every hugely successful manager was once fresh out of school or college, waiting for someone to recognize their talent and offer them a job. They were junior managers looking for promotion, or middle managers hoping it would be them who'd be asked to head up the new project or department or enterprise.

These are the people you want on your team. The raw talent, ready to step up. Never mind about experience – anyone can get that, given time. But you can't fake real talent, brains, energy. When you find someone who has those, offer them the job first and worry about the details later. I'm not talking about mere enthusiasm – sadly lots of untalented people have that – but real ability and an intelligent grasp of the issues they'll be dealing with.

Of course, these talented recruits could eventually outshine you. They could fly up the career ladder and even overtake you. That worries some people. A lot. But it doesn't worry a Rules Player. You see, Rules Players understand that if it says anything about them at all, it will be reflected glory that shines on them. Just like the publisher who offered J.K. Rowling her first contract.

Think about it. These people are going to get to the top with or without you. How much better to be the one who had the per-ception to recognize them, and the sense to hire them, and the privilege to set them on their upward way.

Once you start putting your own team together, the people in it and their performance says more about you as a manager than anything else does. The better the team, the more impressed people will be with you. Hell, some top managers will confess to you that their only real talent has been in hiring people who were smarter than them. They may say it self-deferentially, but actually it's really the only skill you need to get to the top. Know who to hire, and then stay out of their way except to give them what they need to do the job. That doesn't make you a bad manager, it makes you a top-class one, because your team will outperform the rest thanks to your talent-spotting skills.

> **THINK ABOUT IT. THESE PEOPLE ARE GOING TO GET TO THE TOP WITH OR WITHOUT YOU**

Take the rap

Sorry, but if the team screws up, it is entirely your fault. If the team does well, the credit is all theirs. A good manager will always take the rap. I know it's easy to use your team as an excuse, but it won't wash. You are the leader, the manager, the boss. If it all goes pear-shaped you have to stand up and take the flack.

It is very easy to say, 'We didn't meet our targets because . . . ' But you have to say, 'I didn't meet my targets because . . . ' And that 'because' has to be followed by 'I', never 'they'.

It is easy to say, 'We didn't meet our targets because young Brian accidentally upset Client X and they pulled out leaving us short of our sales'. But who put young Brian in charge of such an important client? You. Who organized the sale? You. It has to be you. And your team will die for you if you ask it to, if you take the rap when the going gets tough, believe me. Nothing generates more loyalty than a boss who's prepared to stand up and say, 'I take responsibility'.

> ## IT'S EASY TO USE YOUR TEAM AS AN EXCUSE, BUT IT WON'T WASH

But I also know this is a tough one, really tough to do. It takes self-confidence, courage, trust (that you won't get sacked or disciplined) and a certain maturity.

You might think it will go against you, look as if you are incompetent, but on the contrary. If your boss sees you stand up and say, 'We lost the contract and I take responsibility – these are the steps we're taking to make sure it doesn't happen again', they won't see a failure – they will see a future board member.

RULE 18

Give credit to the team when it deserves it

Just as you must always stand up and take the blame, so too must you always heap praise and credit on your team when things go well. If that fabulous sale to Client X comes off because you happened to stay up all night working on it and then used an old contact from a previous job and then swung it because you happened to know something the competition didn't – why, then you say, 'The team did it'.

Taking the blame does generate loads of loyalty, but so too does giving the team the credit. Say it loudly, in public, sincerely, but do say it. And don't do it tongue in cheek with 'My team did it', as if you are giving it credit but making sure everyone knows who really was responsible. The implication that it is your team isn't necessary. Everyone knows it is your team so there is no need to mention it, ever. It is OK to say, 'It did a great job, it is a fantastic team. I'm incredibly lucky to have it'. This implies you had nothing to do with it and yet everyone knows it is your team and you are its leader so the team will love you and everyone else will think you incredibly humble and self-effacing. Well done you.

Again, all this takes courage and a lot of self-confidence, I know. You work hard and it doesn't seem fair to give the credit away. I know that you really want to stand up and shout, 'Look, it was me, I did this, all by myself, OK?' But you can't.

You see, you didn't do it all by yourself, no matter how much you might believe that. If you are selling, then it is the team that built the product you are selling. Without that team you would have rubbish to sell. Tell the team that selling the product was a doddle because it had done such a good job. It will glow with pride and redouble its efforts.

WITHOUT THAT TEAM
YOU WOULD HAVE
RUBBISH TO SELL

Get the best resources for your team

If your team is a tool you use to get greater glory for little ol' you, then the resources your team uses are the tools it needs to carry it – and thus you – onward and forward. Too many managers think that by cutting their team's resources they are earning some sort of brownie points to be stored up – and used in what? Heaven? I don't think so. You have to get the best resources for your team. By depriving the team you are depriving it also of the chance to shine, to propel you to greater glory.

I know of a lot of managers who say, 'Oh, they can manage for a few more years with Windows Vista'. Or 'They'd probably just play games all day with a new iPhone, I can save a bob or two if I hold off for a bit'. I have even heard, 'I try to keep a short rein on what they need in case it gets out of hand'.

For heaven's sake. Get your team the best, the very, very best, and then let it get on with its job – which is to make you look good.

> GET YOUR TEAM THE BEST,
> THE VERY, VERY BEST, AND
> THEN LET IT GET ON
> WITH ITS JOB

If your people need technology – get it for them even if you have to move heaven and earth. If they need more staff, paper stuff, bigger and better machines, higher quality tools – go get 'em. Whatever it is they need to get their job done slicker, quicker, better, bigger, faster, more productively, cheaper, whatever – go get it. If you have to argue, sweat blood, plead, beg, bust a budget or two – do it. Do it now.

You simply can't expect your team to (a) give of their best, or (b) be motivated, if you keep them short. They will talk to other people you know: colleagues in the same organization, friends in other organizations. They will know when they are being short-changed and they will resent it, resent you and work less effectively. In consequence, you will fail to shine. *Ipso facto* – go get them the best you can.

RULE 20

Celebrate

I find an excuse every day to reward my staff with a little something – a modest celebration for a result no matter how small, how trivial it seems. If you do the same, you'll have a motivated staff who have a habit of celebrating every success. And that's so important.

And the rewards? Tiny. A box of doughnuts. Extra froth on their cappuccinos. A chance to go outside and sit in the sun.

Sometimes I declare today a special day because we just got such and such a result and then I take them out to lunch, let them take time off, let them tell me their worst jokes – never all at the same time, mind.

And, occasionally, I declare such a special day even if we fail to win an order. I reward mistakes, screw-ups, failures, accidents. Why? Well, they've all slogged their guts out, done their best, given their all, sold their grannies and sweated blood. Why shouldn't I reward them? Just because we failed doesn't mean we didn't strive. I am rewarding the effort. I am celebrating all that we did right – effort, struggle, determination, teamwork, drive and good honest labour.

> WHY SHOULDN'T I REWARD THEM? JUST BECAUSE WE FAILED DOESN'T MEAN WE DIDN'T STRIVE

Don't just celebrate the big wins, celebrate all the little ones as well – obviously with smaller celebrations, but celebrations of some sort nevertheless. Hey, any excuse to go and get a coffee. And a bag of doughnuts (or apples if they like). What does that cost you? Very little, but the warm feeling it generates far exceeds any cost.

Keep track of everything you do and say

Now why would you want to do this, unless you're up to no good? No, quite the reverse in fact. The better a manager you are, the more information you need to keep. Why? Two reasons.

First, consistency. You need to keep everything because you will need to check back from time to time. The question, 'Now how did I do this before?' will crop up constantly. Your team needs you to be consistent and you can't be that if you don't remember what you did last time.

If Jim won that big contract last time and you gave him a slap-up lunch and then Terri pulls off a similar deal and you take her out for coffee and a bagel, chances are she's not going to be happy and next time won't give you her very best. So write it down and check back. Similarly if you tell Client X that they are getting the same deal as Client Y, and then they discover that's not true, they will probably take their business elsewhere. Be consistent.

Secondly, proof. Being a good manager, a damn good manager, may open you up to jealousy, resentment and distrust. Not everybody is as upfront as you.

> ## THE BETTER A MANAGER YOU ARE, THE MORE INFORMATION YOU NEED TO KEEP

If your team is giving you 110 per cent and someone else's is only giving them 60 per cent because they are a bad manager, the chances are they will think you're up to something rather than looking at their own poor management skills. It just might be useful to be able to show where successful projects originated, or that you did everything you said you would.

Decisions have to be taken, memos sent, e-mails written, reports presented. Just keep a record of everything. All e-mails should be saved: this is no big deal because computer storage is so immense these days that if all the e-mails ever sent were saved it would still only fill a cyber-eggcup.

Be sensitive to friction

When you are running a team you are dealing with people. And sometimes they take it into their heads to rub each other up the wrong way. Why? Who knows. They just do. They encroach on each other's space, pinch each other's biscuits, take each other's parking spaces. Who starts it? Who knows. Can you let it go on? The hell you can. It has to be nipped in the bud.

You have to be sensitive to friction almost before it begins – and do something about it. There is no point letting it go on for a day longer than it needs to. But to do this you really do need to be on the ball. You have to know your team very well indeed to spot those early warning signs.

If you don't nip it in the bud it will grow into a monster. From tiny nit-picking you'll end up with full-scale war, with the rest of the team taking sides.

What to look out for? Silences when there shouldn't be. Odd complaints: 'God, I wish Clare would stop nattering to me so much.' Grumblings and bitchy gossip. Fierce competitiveness where there doesn't need to be any. Sudden appearance of demarcation lines, such as pot plants to screen desks. Books or computers on desks being used to screen or shield people. People being left out of social invites. People being left out of office humour.

I'm sure you know as much about this as I do and keep your eyes open and your ear to the ground. The secret is stopping it before it gets too bad. Here you have to be diplomat, parent, politician, referee.

You mustn't be seen to be taking sides. You must be seen to be taking swift and resolute action, making it clear that feuding won't be tolerated. Call them in. Reason with them. Separate them. Swap their shifts. Keep them apart. Make them work together as a partnership. There are a whole raft of things you can do, and I'm sure you'll pick the right one at the right time for the right situation.

> ## YOU MUSTN'T BE SEEN TO BE TAKING SIDES. YOU MUST BE SEEN TO BE TAKING SWIFT AND RESOLUTE ACTION

RULE 23

Create a good atmosphere

Creating a good atmosphere isn't only easy but also essential. If your staff are sullen and despondent and depressed and surly – it shows. It shows in their work, the way they handle customers and colleagues, the way they relate to each other and, most importantly, the way they work with you and for you.

It takes nothing to say good morning politely and mean it. It isn't a chore to make sure everyone has got a coffee or tea for a meeting. It takes a second to ask, 'How are you today?' The three rules for any workplace are:

- politeness
- friendliness
- kindness.

Yep, we've all known the bosses who shout and are rude and belligerent, but, like the dinosaurs, they are a dying breed and we can move on. People are entitled to:

- respect
- civilized behaviour
- dignity.

If you can't give them these things you shouldn't be a manager. But I'm sure you can. Creating a good atmosphere is easy. It comes from the top down. It is your job and your responsibility to be cheerful, considerate, polite and helpful. Your people are one of your most important resources – your tools, your weapons of mass achievement. Without them you are nothing. With them you are a team. Use them kindly and don't abuse them. Be genuinely interested in them and their lives. If you don't have time – make time.

I guess the word I am looking for is 'courtesy'. An old-fashioned concept, I'll grant you, but one that gets mountains moved, doors opened and staff working shifts they would normally have refused to do.

> # WITHOUT THEM YOU ARE NOTHING. WITH THEM YOU ARE A TEAM

RULE 24

Inspire loyalty and team spirit

If you work together, chances are you are seeing more of your team than you are of your family. And your team is seeing more of you than of their families. If this is the case you had better all get on. Now you don't have to love each other, but you do have to be a family. And the best way to do that is to inspire loyalty and create a team spirit. You, as the manager, have to be the head of the family.

You have to be respected, looked up to, trusted and relied upon. Tall order. Strong stuff. Can you do all that? Course you can. All you have to do is:

- reward them

- praise them

- be kind to them

- trust them

- inspire them

- lead them

- motivate them

- grow them

- genuinely care about them.

These are the kinds of things that are easier to say than to do, and there's a temptation for you to skip down the list saying 'Yes, yes, I do that'. Now take a minute and go back and really think about each one. Do you *really* do that? Could you do it better? Are you absolutely sure you don't *think* you do it, but perhaps not actually do it? What people think they do and what they actually do can be very different indeed. Find somebody you can ask for honest feedback. Ideally one of your team – if not, somebody who sees you with your team. What do they say you do?

I once worked in competition with another company. One of that manager's team lived with one of my team. She told John, my team member, all her boss's plans, figures, results, future promotions, etc., and I was able to beat him every time. Now why didn't she pass on all my stuff to her boss, seeing as she obviously discussed work with John? Simple. She didn't like her manager. And that was his fault entirely. He was rude to his staff, abusive, unco-operative and unkind. Was I a soft touch? No way. I was strict and businesslike but I treated my team with respect. I didn't have to do much because my competitor was doing enough wrong to make me look good.

> # CHANCES ARE YOU ARE SEEING MORE OF YOUR TEAM THAN YOU ARE OF YOUR FAMILY

RULE 25

Have and show trust in your staff

You have a computer, I take it? OK, it crashes from time to time – that's a given. You have a car. It breaks down from time to time, even if it's only a puncture – that, too, is a given. Now you don't eye either of these warily, expecting them to let you down, watching them like a hawk in case they show any sign of breaking down, do you? No, of course not. So stop watching your staff like that. They are a tool to getting a job done. They will break down, crash, whatever, from time to time but we accept their limitations – Rule 13 – and we allow them to make mistakes – Rule 12 – and we accept that we aren't managing them but their processes instead.

And if you can make that move to trusting your staff you must show them that you are doing exactly that. Trust not only has to be done but it also has to be seen to be done. Sometimes you'll have to make a big show of really leaving them alone to get on with it.

You show them that you trust them by backing off, leaving them alone to get on with the job. Stop peering over their shoulders, checking every few moments, looking up nervously every time they move or cough or get up. Relax and let them get on with it. You can still ask them to report back at the end of the day/week and encourage them to come to you to discuss any problems. Just make it clear you trust them to do it, and you are always there if they need support or guidance.

But, I hear you say, what if I really don't trust them? What if I know they're a lazy, good-for-nothing, shiftless bunch of liberty takers? What if, indeed? Whose team is it? Who employed, trained, kept such a bunch of monkeys?

Sorry, bit harsh, but sometimes we need to face the reality. If you can't trust your team you need to look to your own management skills – or keep reading. A good team leader (that's you) has a good team following them. If the team is faulty, then the leadership has to be challenged – that's not going to be you. If the team is right, you can trust it. If the team really can't be trusted (and are you *sure* about that?) then it needs to be changed.

> YOU SHOW THEM THAT YOU
> TRUST THEM BY BACKING
> OFF, LEAVING THEM ALONE
> TO GET ON WITH THE JOB

Respect individual differences

I have several children. I expect them to operate as a team. But I am also shrewd enough to realize they are all completely different and if I try to treat them all the same, apply the same rules – apart from the discipline ones – I'll get a mutiny, or chaos. Now one of them – and I'm not mentioning any names here but they will know which one I'm talking about – can't be hurried. Not ever, not anyhow. If you shove, he digs his heels in and can't be shifted. He has to be lured, enticed, seduced into being quicker. But I have another son who constantly has to be slowed down. I have to respect – and work with – their individual differences. I simply have to.

Now your team is just the same. Some members can be hurried and others can't. Some will need to be slowed down and others you need to speed up. Some will come to work with a cheery smile, others are best not approached first thing in the morning. Some will be terribly good with technology and others won't. Go back to what Belbin says in Rule 2 and see how everybody in a team has something different to offer – and that difference is what makes your team superb.

With my children if I need something doing fast I know who to call on. If I need a slower, more methodical approach I select another child.

You don't have to let anyone get away with anything just because they are different – keep the discipline rules in place – it's more in the way you treat individual differences, the way you select tasks and the way you expect those tasks to be carried out. We are all different, thank God – a world populated by people like me, even I realize, would be ghastly – and those differences are what make a great team pull together effectively.

So if you're managing a sales team, say, and most of the members are sharp-suited and have slick patter (like you), but one prefers casual garb and is more chatty with his customers, don't mark his cards as 'not a company man' – judge him on the results he gets. If he makes his targets and his customers love him, then *vive la différence*.

> # DIFFERENCES ARE WHAT MAKE A GREAT TEAM PULL TOGETHER EFFECTIVELY

RULE 27

Listen to ideas from others

If you think you know it all, chances are you will be too busy listening to yourself and how great you are to have time to listen to anyone else. But I know that's not you. Everyone, no matter how lowly their position or task, has something to offer you. Try talking to the lift operator, the car park attendant, the canteen staff, the cleaning staff, whoever and whatever. And, most important, listen to people in your team. They are the ones in the know who have to work with the resources and the products. They are the ones at the cutting edge and they may well have ideas, good ideas. You don't need to consult them over every little thing but the big things . . . well, yes. Talk to them. Get their feedback, their ideas, their creativity.

You obviously have to be careful to make sure that although you are listening to them it is you who still carries the can. You might listen but that doesn't mean you are going to act on every one of their ideas. Nip in the bud the feeling that if they suggest, you have to carry out. Therein lies terrible trouble. Listen, assimilate and then decide based on what you've heard, your own experience and ideas and what is practical. It's no good you listening and then not using their information and them becoming terribly despondent – 'What's the use of telling the boss my ideas, they're never used?'

You have to listen without giving the idea that you will necessarily use their ideas, so then they won't be disappointed when you do something completely different. But you can make them think their ideas were incorporated into your overall strategy.

Virtually every team member I have ever known could tell their manager something useful about what they as a team or a company are getting wrong, or how something could be done better. If

you're open to this, ask good questions and listen without preju-
dice (or talking over them), you're immediately in a different class
to most managers.

> # TALK TO THEM. GET THEIR FEEDBACK, THEIR IDEAS, THEIR CREATIVITY

RULE 28

Adapt your style to each team member

Adapting your style does not mean you have to be a chameleon. It means you have to be sensitive to your team's individuality and work with it. You may have outgoing members who like to be praised in public and then you might have quieter, more introspective members who would shrivel up and die if praised in public and prefer to be told they are doing a good job privately. There, you've changed your style without changing your skin, spots or personality.

I have one team member, a very good one, who does her job superbly but who absolutely hates appraisals and would do anything to get out of them. She loathes having to talk about herself in any way – and this borders almost on a real phobia. I have to change my style with her considerably when carrying out a six-monthly appraisal because if she gets wind of the fact that I'm even thinking about doing one she'll hyperventilate and have a panic attack. And then I have another team member who greets me each morning with a very cheery, 'How am I doing, Boss?' Now he really likes talking about himself and would happily be given a daily appraisal – if I were to let it happen. Both team members do their job extremely well – they wouldn't be there if they didn't – but they do need handling in a completely different way. I want them both to continue doing good work, and I have to handle them differently to get the best from them.

Similarly, some people like to be left alone, to create opportunities and make things happen, and they will come and tell you if they need help (the bright self-motivators) and others will need you to direct their actions more and give them specific projects to do. Don't overmanage the former – they'll resist and they'll get irritated (and quite possibly leave). Equally, don't undermanage the latter or they will feel stressed by a lack of structure to their job and won't work hard. Think about the individual. Think about what they need and what motivates them, and adapt your management style accordingly.

YOU HAVE TO BE
SENSITIVE TO YOUR
TEAM'S INDIVIDUALITY
AND WORK WITH IT

RULE 29

Let them think they know more than you (even if they don't)

This one is so simple and yet I bet very few managers use it. And why not? It makes people feel really special and important. All you have to do is say to your staff, 'You know about this, what do you think?' The key principles to this rule are:

- ask their opinion

- get their ideas and views

- give them more responsibility than they ever had before – you'll be surprised how people always rise to a challenge

- discuss important issues and news with them

- encourage feedback

- never dismiss them as being 'mere workers'.

Even if you *know* you know more about a subject than they do – still do it. They feel good. They perform better. They learn from your conversations. Maybe you learn too.

And while you're doing all this, take them through the entire process of your industry so that they don't get stuck in a rut of one department. You have to let them see their important role in the overall scheme of things, how their contribution is valuable and helpful and how the whole thing would flounder without them.

Treat them as you would a valuable client you were showing round. Let them in on your industry's secrets: 'Well, we use the new XP8 coatings on our silicon chips, unlike Mathers and Crowley who still use the old XP5, but I expect you know that anyway, but do keep it under your hat as it's how we stole a march on them and got that huge contract with the DVLA last year.'

Keep them informed about developments in your industry – perhaps you could subscribe to your industry's newsletters and magazines, technical journals and papers, that sort of thing – so that they think you are assuming they are interested, informed, know more than perhaps they do. This will encourage them to keep learning and wanting to know more.

> # ENCOURAGE THEM TO KEEP LEARNING AND WANTING TO KNOW MORE

RULE 30

Don't always have to have the last word

Yes, yes, I know you are the boss, the manager – and a damn good one, may I say – but you don't always have to have the last word. This isn't like being kids in the playground.

If people in your team disagree with you openly, then there are two possible reasons why: either they feel confident enough to engage in debate (in which case you ought to appreciate that) or they are out of line and you aren't imposing discipline enough to stop them. It may well be a warning sign that things are wrong or a sign that things are very right – only you can judge.

If they are out of line and there's a discipline issue, obviously you need to deal with that in private. Otherwise, remember that your staff are grown-ups. You have to give them room to be real people and that means they will sometimes disagree, argue and get cross. That's fine in a good team where people can sound off and nobody takes umbrage. It obviously doesn't work in a poor team.

> REMEMBER THAT YOUR
> STAFF ARE GROWN-UPS.
> YOU HAVE TO GIVE THEM
> ROOM TO BE REAL PEOPLE

It doesn't pay always to have the last word or always to be right or always to correct staff on every little thing. Sometimes, whether they are right or wrong, it's best to let it go. Know the difference between things important enough that you need to have the last word, and things where it really doesn't matter.

RULE 31

Understand the roles of others

I used to believe that to be a good manager I had to be able to do not only my own job – managing – but also everyone else's job as well. And probably, I thought in my heart of hearts, I should be able to do it as well as them if not better. Thus, I figured, if there was an emergency I could step into the breach and do their job and everything would carry on functioning. Yep, I bet you're there before me. If I were to step into their job, who would be doing mine?

Answer, of course: nobody.

The key is to have a practical understanding of what all the jobs entail but realize that you don't need to be able actually to do them. Yes, you do need back-up in the event of a crisis, but it ain't you. You're better off right where you are – managing.

To understand the role, the best way is to know what problems it solves and how it works. But you don't need to be able to do it as well as your team member does – that's what you pay them for. Something about keeping dogs and barking yourself – you need to know what job the guard dog does, but you don't need to go round biting burglars to appreciate it fully.

And often you'll employ someone for such a specialized job you wouldn't know where to begin. You might be the manager of a power plant but you don't need to know how to calculate the shelf life of plutonium. But you do need to know that you employ someone who can do that job for you.

It's also important for all your team to have an understanding of what everyone else does. This certainly helps create a team spirit and a sense of loyalty.

YOU DON'T NEED TO BE
ABLE TO DO A ROLE AS
WELL AS YOUR TEAM
MEMBER DOES – THAT'S
WHAT YOU PAY THEM FOR

Ensure people know exactly what is expected of them

It's easy to give someone a job description and a contract and then sit back and expect them to get on with it. Trouble is, it leads to a lot of confused people and wasted time. Better to let them know right from the off what is expected of them.

And what is expected of them? Well, it's a whole lot more than just the job itself. You have to think through every individual role and what *exactly* is expected of that person.

It's vital that people know what part they play in any strategic plan and what is expected of them as a result. It's essential that team members know the values and standards of the team and the company, and what's expected of them in attitude and behaviour (open? honest? imaginative? caring? can do?). It's also about them being clear on emotional requirements, punctuality, working overtime, behaviour towards colleagues, crisis management – everything.

> LET THEM KNOW RIGHT
> FROM THE OFF WHAT IS
> EXPECTED OF THEM

For new employees this is helped if you have a 'buddy' programme where each new person is linked to someone more experienced who can show them the ropes.

Oh, and some guidelines on relationships at work. It's only fair that everyone knows what is expected of them in any given situation: you can't go rollicking someone for having sex in the broom cupboard if it hasn't been spelt out to them that they don't do that sort of thing – 'But we always did it at my previous place of work and no one complained.'

RULE 33

Have clear expectations

One manager I worked with was very moody. When she was relaxed, everyone was productive but had fun. Occasional high jinx kept their spirits up and she didn't have a problem with it, in moderation. When she was stressed, however, you could get your head bitten off for as little as laughing too loud.

As I say, there were times she was very relaxed. But no one else on her team was. They had no idea what mood she'd be in so they were always on tenterhooks. Would she be happy with a report that was poorly presented but contained all the facts, or would she rather wait until tomorrow and have it looking perfect? Could you get away with the briefest of paperwork for a particular procedure, or did you need to fill it in in triplicate, dotting every i and crossing every t? Hard to say really – it depended which side of the bed she got out of that morning.

And how did her team respond? Well, if you've ever worked for a manager like that, you'll know the answer. They were pretty demoralized, and their standards were hugely inconsistent. Obviously, because their manager's standards were similarly wide-ranging.

Look, if your team don't know what your standards are, how can they aspire to them? They're looking to you to set the lead, and if you don't, they can't tell where they're going or how they're supposed to get there. You have to be consistent in the standards you set and the performance you expect. If something is unacceptable on Monday at 10am, it should be unacceptable on Friday at 4pm. If paperwork is supposed to be filled out a particular way, that's the way it should be done every day of the week.

It may sound unreasonable to have a basic standard and then suddenly, for no consistent reason, to expect more of people. And so it is. But it's just as unfair to let them get away with less just because you're in a particular mood. You're not being nice to them – you're confusing them. And you're failing to ensure your team always produces work of the highest standard. And how fair is it to let one person get away with scrappy presentation when their colleague was expected to produce a polished document last week? No, the only way to ensure good morale among your team, and to make sure it turns in a consistently strong performance, is for you to be consistent in enforcing the standards that you set.

And if you ask me next week, I'll tell you exactly the same.

> # IF SOMETHING IS UNACCEPTABLE ON MONDAY AT 10AM, IT SHOULD BE UNACCEPTABLE ON FRIDAY AT 4PM

RULE 34

Use positive reinforcement motivation

If your staff do something good, tell them. And then tell them again. And again. Keep it up. Put it in writing. Send them a memo – something they can keep. Put it in the company newsletter. Add a note to their file. Whatever, but make it widely known they did good. This is a quick – and cheap (important, with your limited budget) – method of praising and motivating your team (and individual members of course) and it lets everyone know you are monitoring, praising, motivating.

When you praise people, make it simple. If they worked late to get a special order out, say, 'Thank you for working late, we couldn't have done it without you. Your positive response to a difficult situation made everyone's job (especially mine) a lot easier. Thank you'.* That's a whole lot easier than, 'On the evening of the 7th you were seconded to implement an extra shift duty, which you carried out in accordance with our wishes and for which we wish to convey our gratitude, blah, blah . . . '

Let them know why you are thanking them – 'you made my job easier' – rather than just thanking them for what they did – 'you came in for an extra shift'.

Be personal. Use 'I' and 'we', not 'management'. And say 'thank you' in the same way as you would speak. 'I want to thank you' is so much better than 'The management wants to express its gratitude' – who speaks like that?

---

* Reinforce by saying 'thank you' again.

Praise as soon as the job was done, not a week later – do it the next day at the latest. And do it every time people do something beyond their normal brief. If they are asked to work an extra shift every week, that is just a part of their normal working pattern; instead, we are talking here of the extraordinary, the beyond the normal, going that extra mile sort of stuff.

If you reinforce positive behaviour in this way you will almost certainly guarantee it happening again. Fail to notice, to comment, to praise, and chances are your team will stop giving you their best – and who can blame them?

WHEN YOU PRAISE PEOPLE, MAKE IT SIMPLE

Don't try justifying stupid systems

I was travelling on the railway the other day (yes, there are still some of us who do) when we encountered a problem. It was fairly simple. Someone had messed with a security door at the buffet and triggered an alarm – or something. This brought the train to a standstill, probably quite rightly. But it did this in a very long tunnel. The train couldn't move until the fault had been rectified, which involved finding the train manager (they used to be called guards, remember?) and getting him to reset the triggered alarm. All fairly simple.

I was running very late for a meeting, so asked if there wasn't a better system – i.e. letting the buffet staff reset the alarm. The train manager spent about 20 minutes justifying why this system was the best for everyone concerned: him, the buffet staff, the train authorities – everyone, that is, except me, the poor passenger. Much better if he'd just said, 'Yes, it's a useless system and I shall recommend we change it. Thank you for your concern'.

And I bet you have a dozen useless systems within your organization – we all do. Best not try to justify them. If you can't change them, put up with it, get on with it, but don't try hoodwinking the staff into thinking it's all fab. It isn't, and you lose respect and trust if you try convincing people that it's fine when they know it's not.

> ## DON'T TRY HOODWINKING THE STAFF INTO THINKING IT'S ALL FAB

I'm not saying you should go round lamenting loudly everything that is bad about your company – far from it, that road only leads to ruin. Remember, if you can't say something nice, best not to say anything at all. Just don't try justifying something you know is stupid, especially to your team.

RULE 36

Be ready to say yes

The good manager – that's you – tries to stay completely fresh. Not to get stuck in the same old ways of doing things. That means not having a default mechanism of 'No, we don't do it like that'. Instead replace it with 'That's an interesting idea. How do you think that would work?'

What's more, you need to encourage people to come up with new ideas, as well as coming up with them yourself. Try ideas out. Take one new idea each week and give it a go. It might be fairly simple, 'We'd like more choice of biscuits with our morning tea, please', or something radical, 'Listen up, guys, we're going to try a completely new approach to sales and distribution'.

Obviously it makes sense to try out smaller ideas first to make sure your team can cope well with change, and then move on to the more radical ones later. Break 'em in slowly.

And as fast as you are introducing new ideas, get your team to do the same with their own individual jobs so that they don't grow stale either. If everyone has a new idea each week, that's a whole big bunch of new ideas by the end of the year for themselves and for the whole team. 'I just thought I could speed the process up if I . . . ' 'Wow, I could take that idea and adapt it to my work station and then I could . . . ' 'Yeah, and I bet they'd be really interested in this in accounts because it could speed up the whole . . . ' And so on.

Biggest challenge? Getting your team onside – everyone is resistant to change initially. If you flag, the whole team will also flag.

If you maintain the passion, the whole team will be infected and become addicted to this. Believe me. Trust me. I know you already have enough to do, but we'll move on to delegating in a bit and that'll free up some time. Then you'll have more time to do this, which, in a way, is part of your real job – managing.

Encourage innovation. Reward good ideas. Create a culture where ideas are recognized (even if not adopted) and valued.

IF EVERYONE HAS A NEW IDEA
EACH WEEK, THAT'S A WHOLE
BIG BUNCH OF NEW IDEAS BY
THE END OF THE YEAR

RULE 37

Train them to bring you solutions, not problems

It's terribly easy for staff to moan. I think it becomes a habit. You have to train your staff not just to moan. You can allow moaning but insist that if they bring you a problem they must also suggest a solution to the problem. Any idea that there is something wrong should always be met with, 'And what would you like me to do about it?' If they complain, meet them with, 'What do you think we should do?'

The best manager I ever worked for carried this even further and made us tell him the solution first – and then let him guess what he thought our 'problem' was. It made it a game, which was sort of fun, but it also made us think on our feet a bit – made us be a bit lateral in our moaning. I was having a problem with security staff. I thought they were wiping the CCTV footage without watching it, which was not on. This was my problem because if anything had happened I would have carried the can. I needed them to watch carefully but couldn't devise a solution to this problem – but I couldn't just go to the boss and moan that they weren't doing their job properly. I had to come up with a solution first.

Then it dawned on me that I didn't need to go to the boss. I could solve this one myself. I had to make sure the security staff thought there was something worth watching. I mentioned that some members of staff had been reported as having sex somewhere on the premises and it could have been covered by the CCTV cameras, but no one was sure by which camera. There were cameras covering car parks, offices, corridors and storage areas in the basement. Result. The security bods started watching as if their lives depended on it. My boss was pleased because this was part of my job brief and he had noticed it wasn't being done properly and was going to pull me up on it. And I had come up with a solution to a problem without going to my boss and just moaning, 'Oh, the security people aren't doing their job properly . . . '

Admittedly I had to come up with a fresh solution once the security staff realized they weren't going to see any smutty pictures – but it took them a long time, and they kept going back just in case . . .

ANY IDEA THAT THERE IS SOMETHING WRONG SHOULD ALWAYS BE MET WITH, 'AND WHAT WOULD YOU LIKE ME TO DO ABOUT IT?'

MANAGING
YOURSELF

So those are the basic Rules for managing a team. And obviously most managers have a team to manage. But all managers have themselves to manage as well – that's you. So the next set of Rules is for you. These are Rules to help you become more effective as well as more efficient. It's hard enough just getting through the day without trying to improve as well – believe me, I know.

Being a manager is a tough job because it is always two jobs at once. You have to get your own work done and also be looking out for a team. The higher up the scale we go, the further away from our original job we get. And often no one bothers to train us as to what the new job – management – actually entails. Sure, we go on the odd course – and some are very odd: I speak as one who has made LEGO® bridges, done jigsaws that are face down, been on canoeing weekends and all in the name of management training – but we don't specifically train to be managers. Management is something we sort of pick up as we go along. Sure, there are a few good instinctive managers, but invariably we stumble along picking up the odd hint and clue here and there – it's a very hit and miss operation.

And a lot of what we are taught is fairly obvious. What I'm doing here is giving you the unwritten stuff – the stuff you don't get on those canoeing weekends.

Work hard

The fundamental Rule of management, I'm afraid, is get the basic job done, get it done well and work bloody hard at it. No good being a fantastic people manager if you let the basic job slip. You may have to get into the office earlier than anyone else, earlier than you've ever got there before, but get in early you must.

Once you have cleared your work out of the way you can concentrate on managing your team. Paperwork has to be done efficiently and on time. This isn't the place to go into lengthy training sessions on time management and the like, but basically you will have to be:

- organized
- dedicated
- ruthlessly efficient
- focused.

No choice, I'm afraid. You have to knuckle down and get on with it. Management isn't swanning around issuing orders and looking cool. It's actually about what goes on in the background – the work being done where no one sees it.

And if you want to know if you are being a good manager now – take a look at your desk. Go on. Right now. What do you see? Clear space and order? Paper everywhere and piles of unsorted stuff? Do the same with your briefcase, files, computer even. Order or disorder?

> ## YOU HAVE TO KNUCKLE DOWN AND GET ON WITH IT

You have to use whatever tools you have to hand to make sure the work is done, done well, and done on time. Make lists, use pop-up calendars on your computer, delegate, seek help, stay up late, get up early, get up earlier. Obviously you still need to refer to Rule 75: Go home – you have to have a life. But get that work done and learn to be ruthlessly efficient.

RULE 39

Set the standard

If you slouch in late, argue with your customers, are disrespectful and produce shoddy work, chances are your team is going to go to hell in a handcart. If, on the other hand, and I assume this is more likely the case, you arrive not only on time but early, do your work well and on time (see Rule 38), behave like a decent, honest, civilized human being and use your talent, chances are your staff will go to the top.

Everyone needs someone to look up to, someone they can respect and want to emulate. Sorry, matey, but that someone is you. Tough call, I know. If you think heroes are so out of date, old-fashioned and redundant, then think again. Every one of your team has a special relationship with you. You are their leader, their inspiration, their boss (there's a word to make you shudder, but that's what you are), their mentor, guide, teacher, hero, role model, champion, defender, guardian. To be all these things means you have to set an example. You have to play the part. You have to set standards. You have to be that role model.

The bottom line is: if you don't care, why should they? You've got to set an example in everything you do. Think before you speak. Consider how you react. 'Do as I say, not as I do' doesn't work. Be what you want to see in them.

You've also got to go beyond that and raise their stakes. You've got to give your staff something to aspire to, something to want to raise themselves up to. That's you.

Ideally, you'll have some style, some flair, some spark of originality that will set you apart from the herd – we're thinking Lauren Bacall and Cary Grant here, not Meat Loaf and early Madonna.*

---

* No offence, both make really good albums and are superb rock stars but as role models for managers they don't cut the mustard.

You've got to look the part, act the part, do the part – method acting here: feel the manager, think the manager, be the manager.

> # YOU'VE GOT TO GIVE YOUR
> # STAFF SOMETHING
> # TO ASPIRE TO

RULE 40

Enjoy yourself

I'm going to be blunt now. If you're not enjoying what you do, then get the hell out and make room for someone who is going to enjoy it. Rule 41 may put things into context, but for the moment we need to get you feeling good about what you're doing.

Enjoying work is about taking pleasure in a job well done, having an inner smile, finding something to laugh about and not taking it *too* seriously (no, this does not mean you laugh *at* people or fail to do your job to the very highest standards).

Enjoying work is about seeing your job, your role, in a much bigger context. You can be hardworking and you can enjoy yourself – you can do both. You can be productive, effective, efficient, industrious, sober, reliable and responsible – and yet still be having fun. It's your choice. No one told you that you had to be grave and uptight. All you were hired to do was your job.

The best bit is that if you learn when to be serious and when to let up and find humour in a situation it will have a magical effect on those around you.

> ## NO ONE TOLD YOU THAT YOU HAD TO BE GRAVE AND UPTIGHT. ALL YOU WERE HIRED TO DO WAS YOUR JOB

And if you work in a place where serious and uptight is the norm, here is a secret just for you: no one knows what is going on inside your head. No one. Just so long as the exterior is what they want, the inside can be whatever you want.

Don't let it get to you

If it all gets too much, remember it's just a job. Sure, one we care about and try to do to the very best of our ability. One we worry about and think about when we're not at work. One we would like to make better and improve and be more effective at.

But it is only a job when all is said and done.

Look around you. You'll see the ones who think that what they do is central to the Earth's movement or vital to the well-being of the entire planet. Nothing could be further from the truth. Enjoy it by all means. Take it seriously and give it all you've got, but remember it is just a job and it can be replaced, you can be replaced, the world will go on.

If the job is stressful in a way you don't like, think about something in life that is more important to you. Your kids, your dog, your mum. Your weekend hang-gliding trips. I don't know what you do when you're not at work, but find something that *really* matters, and use it to help you get through those bad times at work. Use it to get some perspective and recognize that there are more important things than your job.

You can even daydream about these important things to get you through the working day – so long as you promise you'll only do it when you're not supposed to be concentrating on the job. But meal breaks, walking over to another building, even when you go to the loo, are times you can stop for a moment and remind yourself of what matters in life.

And of course you should also spend time thinking about why work is getting you down, and coming up with some kind of plan for improving things. Do you need to cut down your hours, resolve the festering feelings between team members, clinch a particular contract, complete your next budget?

Well, get on with it if that's the case, and then you can get back to enjoying the job.

Not letting it get to you doesn't mean not caring or not taking pride and pleasure in what you do. No, it means putting things into context so you can go home and switch off. Don't let it eat away at you, make you unhealthily stressed or overwrought.

> NOT LETTING IT GET TO YOU
> DOESN'T MEAN NOT CARING
> OR NOT TAKING PRIDE AND
> PLEASURE IN WHAT YOU DO

RULE 42

Know what you are supposed to be doing

So what are you supposed to be doing? It's very easy to think you know, but do you really? It's like when your boss says, 'I want this done as soon as possible'. Now that's really easy, isn't it? Well, actually no. As soon as whose idea of possible? Yours? The boss's? And does 'want' imply a wish or a need? And 'done' is open to all sorts of interpretation.

I know I'm being picky and pedantic but I'm illustrating a point here. You know you have a team and you have to manage it. You know you have budgets and figures and targets and they all have to be met. You know you have a forward-looking strategy and you would like to implement that. You know you have a contract and a job description.

But what are you supposed to be doing? What's your priority? What's the end point? What's the goal? Has anything changed recently (senior management sometimes have a way of changing their minds and expecting you to know telepathically)?

I once worked for a senior manager who, to all outward appearances, wanted my team to be successful and productive but who seemed to be hampering my every move. Whenever I wanted to make changes that would drastically improve our figures he hesitated and delayed and wouldn't make a decision. I couldn't figure out what I was supposed to be doing. I wanted to run the department for him as well as I could, but he seemed to be putting obstacles in my path.

Eventually I discovered that another department – run by a relative of his – was supposed to be the winning team. I wasn't allowed to be the golden boy because that was the role for his young nephew. He wanted me to fail so young Sam could look good. I was supposed to be useless. Once I had that info – what I was supposed to be doing – I could work effectively with it. You've got to know what you're supposed to be doing.

> # WHAT'S YOUR PRIORITY?
> # WHAT'S THE END POINT?
> # WHAT'S THE GOAL?

RULE 43

Know what you are actually doing

So what are you doing? Important but overlooked rule, this one. Go on, answer the question, what are you doing?

To answer this you need to have long- and short-term plans formulated. If you haven't got a plan, you don't have a map. If you don't have a map, you'll never find the treasure. In *Pirates of the Caribbean: The Curse of the Black Pearl*, when someone questions his ability to sail his ship with only two men, Johnny Depp needs no other answer than he's Captain Jack Sparrow. 'Savvy?' If you know who you are and where you are going, you are indeed a pirate and clearly so.

So, are you laying the groundwork for future promotion? Marking time until you decide what to do? Counting down the days until you retire? Collecting information so you can go to a rival and use it profitably? Waiting to be head-hunted? Learning more about the industry so you can make a sideways move? Enjoying yourself and having a ball? Doing a hatchet job for the management and making a third of the workforce redundant?* Trying hard to be noticed by senior management? Working hard just to do a good job and stay ahead of the game? Building a social network to have fun with? Stealing ideas, resources, staff and machinery to start your own rival business? (Oh, I've seen this done, and a very successful job they made of it too – they knew exactly what they were doing.)

---

* I knew a general manager of a big engineering concern who was brought in from the USA to do exactly that – and the workforce knew it. His first mass meeting was greeted with boos and catcalls. He stood his ground and just said, 'I am not the enemy here. The enemy is the downturn in business. I am not the enemy so don't shout at me'. Worked like a charm.

There are no right and wrong answers. Well, actually a wrong answer would be, 'I haven't a clue'. You have to know what it is you are *actually* doing. Not what you are *supposed* to be doing. Not what you *want* to be doing. Not what the company *thinks* you are doing. But what you are *actually* doing. Once you know that you can work miracles because you have secret knowledge. Perhaps everyone else also knows; perhaps no one else knows. But *you* know and that is the important thing.

Now have a quick look round at your team and tell me what each and every one is actually doing. Good exercise.

IF YOU HAVEN'T GOT A PLAN,

YOU DON'T HAVE A MAP.

IF YOU DON'T HAVE A MAP,

YOU'LL NEVER FIND

THE TREASURE

Value your time

I once sat in a meeting, as a very junior manager, in which there was an interminable discussion going on about whether or not we should buy a particular piece of equipment that some people thought too pricey. I'd said what I had to say on the subject (as indeed had everyone, but some of them were saying it several times) so to pass the time I did a quick, back-of-the-envelope calculation of the combined hourly rate of everyone sitting round the table. I pretty much knew everyone's salaries, so it would have been a fairly close estimate. The interesting thing was that the half hour we spent talking about this piece of equipment was nearly twice as costly as the thing itself.

As a Rules manager, you need to know what your time is worth, and then keep it in the forefront of your mind all the time. The calculation is easy of course – divide your yearly salary into 52 weeks, and then each week into however many hours you're employed for. The trickier bit – until you're in the habit – is remembering to check if what you're doing is a valuable use of your time.

Remember that for many organizations, the wages bill is the largest single chunk of outgoings. Even when it's not, it's still a significant figure. And it's one that you have control over, at least when it comes to you. So you need to ensure that whatever you're doing is a good investment of that bit of your time. If not, you need to be ruthless cutting it out.

You know those people who waste your time? They're also wasting your employer's money, which could be used more effectively by you doing something else. So it's your duty to deal firmly with them (but politely of course).

And you must be just as firm with yourself when you catch yourself procrastinating, filling in time, waiting around, doing pointless stuff, chatting with colleagues, working inefficiently, and so on. Your organization is trusting you to invest their money (i.e. your salary) as profitably as possible. Don't let them down.

This is also a useful exercise to go through when your time is pulled in more than one direction. Should you go to this meeting, or get that report finished? Well, which is going to produce the greater return on investment? That should give you your answer.

> YOUR ORGANIZATION IS TRUSTING YOU TO INVEST YOUR SALARY AS PROFITABLY AS POSSIBLE. DON'T LET THEM DOWN

Be proactive, not reactive

I know, I know, it takes you all your time just to get the job done, the paperwork tidied and the plants watered without having to think about the future or be a whiz innovator. But the smart manager – that's you again – puts aside 30 minutes a week for forward planning. Try asking yourself simple questions: 'How can I generate more sales?' 'What can I do more expediently?' 'How could I cut staff turnover?' 'How can I convert more leads to sales?' 'How could I streamline the accounting procedure?' 'How could I move into another sector?' 'How could I get my team to work harder, faster, brighter?' 'How could I get them to brainstorm more freely?' 'How could I hold meetings that wouldn't waste so much time?'

There is an old saying, 'If you always do what you've always done, you'll always get what you've always got'. And by golly it's true. If you aren't proactive you'll stagnate. And if you do that the crocodiles will bite your bum. You have to keep paddling, keep moving forwards in the water. Sharks have to keep moving forwards all their life to keep water passing through or over their gills. They never stop. Be a shark. Keep moving forwards. Because if you don't there will be plenty of others willing to do so.

And believe me, I know what it's like. You open your mail box and there are loads of e-mails to deal with. Then there's the post. Then there are the staff issues. Then there's lunch. Then there's the afternoon work to be done and then there's a panic to get all the post ready to go out and then there's a quick cup of tea and then it's about time to pack it all in and go home and there's this idiot telling me I've got to take 30 minutes out of a jam-packed day to think about the future. Yeah, in your dreams.

But those 30 minutes can be combined with another task. Once a week I have lunch on my own and spend the time being proactive, thinking about the future, thinking of ways to be one jump ahead of the competition. But I do have to go out alone for that lunch or people come and interrupt my mental planning session.

BE A SHARK.

KEEP MOVING FORWARDS

RULE 46

Be consistent

If you were to wear a smart business suit every day and then suddenly, without warning, turn up in denim and a worn T-shirt, chances are people would look at you askance.*

If you turn in good work and then one day hand in a pile of rubbish, people are going to think you've blown it.

If you treat the staff courteously until one day you blow your top and shout at everyone, they won't trust you any more.

If you usually get in early and then one day stroll in around noon smelling of beer, they will stop taking you seriously and accuse you of being a drunk.

> ## IF YOU TURN IN GOOD WORK AND THEN ONE DAY HAND IN A PILE OF RUBBISH, PEOPLE ARE GOING TO THINK YOU'VE BLOWN IT

People need to know what to expect from you. You have to be consistent. You have to treat all staff the same. Do your work the same. You must avoid drawing the spotlight of gossip down on

---

* Try it, it's fun. If you don't know what *askance* is, look it up and then try it.

you. You must be blameless, above reproach (that's probably the same thing), honest, reliable and dependable (again that's probably the same thing).

But you don't have to be grey or dull or boring. You can be exciting, dynamic, stylish, adventurous, innovative, challenging – just make sure that whatever it is you decide to be, you stick at it and be consistent consistently.

Set realistic targets for yourself – no, really realistic

We're not talking budgets here or corporate targets. We're talking personal goals, personal objectives, personal bottom lines. You have to set them or you won't be able to determine whether or not you are a success. There's no point, by the way, in judging yourself against anyone else. I always wanted to be terribly good at sport but I can't run and fail miserably. It had always led me to believe I was a failure, but I found out the other day that there is a gene for good sporting skills and it is one I obviously don't have. Am I a failure? Nope, just genetically challenged, and I can't beat myself up about that. I am good at other things and I measure my success against:

- how I was doing last year
- how I was doing five years ago
- how I'm doing against my personal targets
- how I'm doing against my long-term plan.

There isn't another person in sight because measuring yourself against anyone else is a mug's game.

I once owned a motorbike – a rather grand one and I loved it very much. I came alongside another motorcyclist at the traffic lights and looked his bike over. 'That's the one I want', I cried to myself in the splendid isolation of my crash helmet. He was looking at my bike and obviously thinking the same thing. As the lights changed and we both roared away together I realized he and I were riding identical bikes. Ah, the fickle mind, how it winds us up, beats us up and plays tricks. Look at anyone and chances are there will be something to envy, but you don't know what goes on inside them. Walk a mile in someone else's shoes, they say, and chances are you'll be a mile away; but you've got their shoes, make a run for it.

So set yourself some targets but be realistic about them. 'I'm going to be Emperor of the World' may sound impressive but it is totally unrealistic (unless you're an American president perhaps?).

Make your targets challenging but attainable, realistic but a bit of a struggle – no good making them too easy, or too hard.

AH, THE FICKLE MIND, HOW IT WINDS US UP, BEATS US UP AND PLAYS TRICKS

RULE 48

Have a game plan, but keep it secret

No one knows what goes on inside your head. No one knows what lofty heights you aspire to. No one knows what you're really up to – remember Rule 43: Know what you are actually doing – so you can work on your game plan and be doing your job well at the same time. Your game plan should incorporate both long- and short-term goals – where you want to be, where you intend being – and then you have something to match your success against – where you actually are.

> ## YOUR GAME PLAN SHOULD INCORPORATE BOTH LONG- AND SHORT-TERM GOALS

Why keep it secret? Because the game plan of your corporation, your management team and your boss may not exactly match your own game plan. This is a personal game plan and should be kept to yourself to protect your dreams and hopes and aspirations – there is nothing quite like having someone dampen your fireworks. An awful lot of management is about having front – being able to look the part, to inspire confidence, to walk your walk. If people get wind of any game plan that deviates from that confident air of the perfect manager they will lose confidence. You might be thinking of striking out on your own, but don't tell anyone or they will assume you are leaving any minute now, even if your plans don't allow for that for several years. If you have a game plan of rapid promotion, people will assume you are a high flyer and stop giving you long-term projects on the grounds that you'll be moving up too soon. And so on. Play your cards close to your chest and keep up the appearance of dedication, commitment, reliability, diligence and stability – even if in your heart of hearts you are planning revolution, climbing Everest or taking over the empire.

RULE 49

Get rid of superfluous rules

Ha, I can hear you thinking, 'He's shot himself in the foot now. Get rid of superfluous rules, ha, in a book of rules?' Yep, get rid of superfluous rules. Not my rules of course, not your rules of course. Their rules, obviously. Let people in your team know that you are on their side and will streamline any procedures to enhance efficiency. That means old baggage has to go.

In any workplace there will be a mountain of red tape, bureaucracy, old rules left in place from previous management regimes – get rid of them all. Question everything you and your team do and make it work slicker and quicker by getting rid of anything that is redundant, unnecessary, left over. This is the work equivalent of clutter clearing, process feng shui if you like.

It's terribly easy to settle into a routine and to stop seeing things with a clear eye, a fresh vision. Every day you have to go into work and see it as an outside consultant would. Question 'Why do we do this? Why do we do it like this?' I bet you'll find a lot of clutter and can eliminate it.

> ## WHY DO WE DO THIS?
> ## WHY DO WE DO IT LIKE THIS?

I once worked for a company where every letter going out had to be 'vetted' by a senior office secretary. She was a bit of a dragon to say the least and if you ever got on the wrong side of her your letters went straight to the bottom of the pile – and stayed there. Why did letters have to be routed through her? Beats me, but I had to work unbelievably hard to get rid of that bit of Dickensian nonsense.

Streamline. Save time. Make your people happier and more trusted. Simple really.

RULE 50

Learn from your mistakes

We all make mistakes – we wouldn't be the wonderfully creative, innovative managers we are if we didn't. But some managers gloss over any mistakes they make. They cover them, bury them, forget about them.

You, as a brilliant manager, won't do that. You won't beat yourself up over them, nor sit in a pit of misery over them but you will analyze what went wrong, discuss with colleagues why it went wrong and make a plan to prevent it from going wrong again.

Our mistakes could be anything from a badly handled appraisal, a lost sale, a badly thought-out report, a poor use of time or resources, a failure to meet a deadline – when you start to write down how many failures there could be the list is endless.

Once you have made your mistake the important thing to do as well as all the above is to find out the right way to do it next time.

Being a manager is an ongoing learning experience. You never stand still and you never think you know it all – you don't and can't. But you can have trusted people to ask and good reference books to hand to guide you – especially if they are short, sharp, snappy, and practical.*

Mistakes are brilliant because they not only teach us where we went wrong but also how to fix it. You are a better manager, more experienced, have a wider spectrum to call on when you've made a few errors. We all make mistakes – admit them, learn from them and move on.

---

* See, for example, *Fast Thinking Manager's Manual* by Ros Jay (Pearson Education, 2nd edition, 2004).

BEING A MANAGER IS AN ONGOING LEARNING EXPERIENCE

Be ready to unlearn – what works, changes

You know how it is, you're sailing along doing what you've always done and suddenly you're not making your figures, sales are dropping, staff turnover is going up, things are falling apart. But you're not doing anything you haven't done in the past. You had a winning formula and suddenly it doesn't work any more. What can you do? Well, for a start realize that what works, changes. And it can change so rapidly you didn't realize it until it's too late. Be aware of this, be ready and prepared to adapt quickly. You have to stay abreast of:

- latest innovations in your industry

- new technology

- new terminology

- new methodology

- changes in sales, market trends, staff turnover figures, targets and budgets.

Don't get stuck in any ruts. Be ready to spin on a coin if you have to. Good management is about adapting to change rapidly and skilfully. If you don't, you go the way of the dinosaurs.

> GOOD MANAGEMENT IS ABOUT ADAPTING TO CHANGE RAPIDLY AND SKILFULLY

The same goes for all sorts of things – style of management with staff, for instance. You might have a way with them that has worked for years and all of a sudden it doesn't. You could persevere, but you might lose staff rapidly. Better to be ready to unlearn your old ways and adopt new ones. It could be you have changed, unknowingly, unconsciously. If we get stuck in ways of doing things, sometimes we change them without recognizing that change. We have to be alert to those changes that creep in.

Cut the crap – prioritize

I used to work for a manager who was fond of asking who we worked for. If we said ourselves, he shook his head. If we said him, he shook his head. If we said the directors, he shook his head. And on and on. The only answer, he said, was the shareholders. And the only reason we worked, he said, was for the profit. Everything else was padding. Fair enough. We do work for the shareholders – whoever they might be. It might be yourself if you are a one-person band. They might be the directors if it's a family-owned firm and not trading on the stock market. They might be millions of little people who have all invested.

So cut the crap. There is only one reason for being in business, no matter what anyone says – profit. To make money. If you're making your figures, good. If you're not, clear your desk out. Simple. Now you have a neat yardstick to judge everything you do. Ask, 'Does this contribute towards the profits I am making, or not?' If it does, keep right on doing it. If it doesn't, chuck it out.

When all is said and done, that is what it's all about. No money, no business. No business, no job. No job, no mortgage, car, bread on the table, holidays in Tuscany.

> ## NO MONEY, NO BUSINESS.
> ## NO BUSINESS, NO JOB

I bet if you sit down and look at everything you do, a lot of it will be padding. Time to prioritize. Cut the crap and dedicate yourself to one thing and one thing only – the bottom line. And that's what separates a really sharp manager like you from all the others. That clear focus, that vision, that dedication.

RULE 53

Cultivate those in the know

Always remember it's not who you know, but whom you know. And in business there are movers and shakers and there are worker ants. You need to know who the movers and shakers are – and cultivate them. Often senior management have PAs that act as guards – you don't get to talk to God but you do get to be brushed off by God's right-hand PA. You have to get on the right side of the PA and that means charm and politeness, tact and discretion, gamesmanship and ruthless cunning.

I once worked for a boss who used a business consultant as his sort of unofficial PA – she shielded and protected him from having to talk to his staff. Her surname was Burton and everyone called her Mrs Burton except those in the boss's inner circle who called her JB.

I started to call her JB also and the first few times she looked at me quite horrified – I was only a junior manager and not entitled to do so. But I got away with it. After a few weeks the boss heard me call her JB and assumed I had been accepted into her inner circle of close chums and colleagues. He started to give me more responsibility, which meant she started to give me respect as I was obviously one of his favourites – and they bounced off each other, each believing me to be the other's accepted one and I got preferential treatment from both.

Lots of people think that (a) the 'old school tie' system is dead, or (b) if it ain't dead it ought to be, or (c) it is dead and therefore a new system has taken its place and having to know those in the know no longer counts, and/or (d) raw talent will always shine through.

Some of the above may be true. The old school tie thing will never be dead because those in the know are the ones who still run that particular club. It might not be school any more, instead it might be the golf club, charity work, breakfast clubs, university, family, previous places of work, old friends, whatever. People in the know like to collect round them people they also know and therefore can trust. You have to get to know those around those who need to be known: cultivate them, then become one of those around those in the know – and then become one of those in the know. What you do then is entirely up to you.

> # YOU NEED TO KNOW WHO THE MOVERS AND SHAKERS ARE – AND CULTIVATE THEM

Know when to kick the door shut

Keeping an open-door policy as a manager is a basically good idea, but there comes a time when you have to know it is time to kick the door shut so that you can:

* get on with some work

* have a meeting in private

* let your team know you don't want to be disturbed

* let the team know you really are the boss and not really one of them at all.

Obviously a good manager such as yourself likes to have an open-door policy so that the staff have access to you when and as they need. But there are times when it is necessary physically and psychologically to create a barrier. You see, the real secret of good management is that no matter how chummy you are with the team there comes a time when it is essential that you are actually the boss.

Ruling by democracy is all very well; meetings and committees are fine; joint discussions are rewarding. But when push comes to shove you have to be prepared to carry the can and that means you have to fly by the seat of your pants, make the tough calls and be the boss. And occasionally shutting the door reinforces that. You don't have to be a cruel or harsh or dictatorial boss, but a boss you must be.

If you are one of those managers who finds it hard to be assertive or 'bossy', I suggest you practise kicking the door shut. It is a deeply symbolic gesture about who controls your environment – you. Do it a few times and the team will get the message. Once you've got used to it you can control who sits down in your office and how long they stay. It is essential for employees to take you seriously, for you to stamp your authority on the situation. Kicking the door shut symbolizes you are the manager – and this is a good thing, believe me. Oh, and it'll also mean you get some work done without interruption. Just don't do it too often – nothing is more frustrating than a boss who is never available.

> ## THERE ARE TIMES WHEN IT IS NECESSARY PHYSICALLY AND PSYCHOLOGICALLY TO CREATE A BARRIER

RULE 55

Fill your time productively and profitably

Once you've learnt to kick the door shut you'll find yourself alone in an empty office. But to be the really great and effective manager you are, and are going to be, you don't coast or cruise. You get your head down and get the work done. And you get it done fast and effectively and efficiently. Then you do some work on your long-term goals, your game plan and your business education (don't stand still – read something).

Working hard when you're not being encouraged with an electric cattle prod is a bit like working for yourself. You have to be motivated, dedicated and focused. It takes practice and training. We all like to goof off. And that's fine every now and then. We all need thinking time, down time. It is important, though, not to overdo it.

Don't let the time bandits come in and steal a whole day. Set little deadlines. Make short lists so you can cross off lots and feel good about what you've done. Get loads of fresh air, or you'll sleep too much. Don't drink alcohol at lunchtime, or you'll sleep afternoons. Go to bed early enough, or you'll be trying to catch up on sleep in the office.

Beware time-wasting people. Practise telling people you've got something important and urgent to finish and can you come and see them later?

Beware e-mails too – they have a way of sucking time. And they tend to make you terribly reactive – 'Oh, I've got a clear in-box, all my work is done.' But the truth is, work isn't replying to e-mails or composing e-mails – it is getting your sleeves rolled up and actually doing something: making phone calls, chasing people, creating sales, checking production, filing reports. Get on with it, now. Be productive. Be profitable. Everything else can take a hike.

DON'T STAND STILL – READ SOMETHING

Have a Plan B and a Plan C

You have to plan for disasters. You've got to build a 'what if' clause into everything you do. If you don't, you'll be caught looking inept. Never assume it's all going right – it isn't. Never assume you'll always do OK – you won't. Never assume technology will always work – it won't. Never assume you've got enough time – you haven't. Never assume they'll turn up on time – they won't. Never assume you won't forget things – you will. Never assume Plan A will work – it won't. Never assume Plan B will also work – one day that won't either.

I think you might get the picture by now. When things go wrong – and they will – be ready to improvise, adapt and overcome. Say you're giving a presentation and have mapped out the whole thing using PowerPoint. What will you do if there is a power cut? Technology failure? You must have worked out beforehand what to do when power fails or technology screws up or that order fails to come in – because they will. Maybe not today, but tomorrow lies waiting to catch you unawares, unguarded, unprepared.

> ## NEVER ASSUME YOU'VE GOT ENOUGH TIME – YOU HAVEN'T

Really good managers, of course, don't need Plan B or Plan C because they can think on their feet and are ready to cover their tracks at any time, ready to improvise. I think it wiser, though, constantly to ask, 'How am I going to cope when this doesn't work?' Serves me every time.

Capitalize on chance – be lucky, but never admit it

If you keep your eyes open and your wits about you there will be opportunities, chances, bits of random luck. If you are quick and clever and enterprising you can catch the coat-tails of such moments and ride on the back of them. Such is luck. Grab it while you can, because it is a fleeting thing. You can't build it into a plan or a budget or a report, but it will happen all around you. In fact, the more you cherish it and nurture it and look for it, the more it will happen. We have to believe in luck or otherwise how could we attribute the success of people we don't like?

Now don't go building your career on luck, it doesn't work like that. I'm saying we all get a bit lucky from time to time and when that happens you have to hang on in there and go with it – and then keep quiet about it. You don't always have to tell the truth – and all that false modesty sucks. If you were lucky, say, 'It was a lucky break', but say it in such a way that people know months of careful planning went into it, years of research, decades of experience – because that, frankly, is the truth.

There is no such thing as luck alone, but there are random-seeming moments of opportunity which you can grasp because of all that work, experience, research, planning. If you fail to grasp, the moment will fly past and you'll be none the better for it. But learn to recognize and capitalize on the opportunity, and you can hitch a ride on it. It's all down to you. If you weren't so good at your job, the luck wouldn't happen. If you weren't such a good manager, you wouldn't be quick enough to seize those moments and utilize them.

As US President Thomas Jefferson said, 'I am a great believer in luck, and I find the harder I work the more I have of it'.

> # IF YOU WEREN'T SO GOOD AT YOUR JOB, THE LUCK WOULDN'T HAPPEN

RULE 58

Recognize when you're stressed

The good manager stays well ahead of the stress game. And why? Because stress is counterproductive – it isn't profitable. The old image of the stressed executive popping pills, with high blood pressure but still pulling off fantastic deals is just that – old. The modern executive is laid back, unhurried, charming, thoughtful, careful, on top of their job. You don't need stress. You really, really don't. Yes, you need excitement, challenge, enthusiasm, exhilaration and stimulation, but you do not need stress.

Stress is just excitement and fun that has gone wrong. Instead of loving your job, you start to fear it. Instead of being excited, you experience fear. Instead of challenge, it's confrontation.

So how do you manifest stress? No really, how do you experience it? This is such a personal thing. I know when I'm under a lot of stress because I shout more, reason less, demand more, am polite less, rush more, am laid-back less. But that's me. For you it might be smoking or drinking more or not sleeping or not eating (or eating too much or too hurriedly or too much junk food) or it might show as nervous exhaustion (sleeping too much), panic attacks, twitches, tics, irrational fears, inappropriate behaviour, driving too fast (me again as well to that one). If you don't know what your signs are, ask somebody who knows you well – they will be able to tell you.

When I notice a couple of my stress symptoms I take time out to check:

- why I am stressed
- what is causing the stress
- what I can do about it
- how I can stop it recurring again.

I don't like being stressed (my children say I am a real pain) and there is no job worth doing that I'm going to allow to affect my health detrimentally. I know how to chill – I'm very good at lowering the stress levels once I notice they've crept up. I know what works for me. What works for you?

> # YES, YOU NEED EXCITEMENT, CHALLENGE, ENTHUSIASM, EXHILARATION AND STIMULATION, BUT YOU DO NOT NEED STRESS

Manage your health

It's easy to put off managing your health. Do it now. The general advice is:

- eat properly – sitting down in a relaxed setting, taking time to enjoy your food

- eat proper food – fresh, organic, lean meat, fresh fruit, salads, vegetables, roughage, no junk, no processed food

- get a decent night's sleep – every night

- stop worrying – laugh, have fun, enjoy something not work-related

- carry out basic health checks regularly to catch major conditions in time, such as testicular or breast lumps and bumps

- work in a comfortable and safe environment

- get yourself screened from time to time for cholesterol levels, blood pressure, etc.

- have supportive and loving relationships

- have some sort of belief system to sustain you in times of crisis

- exercise

- watch your weight

- drink moderately

- don't smoke.*

---

* Of all of them, this is the biggie apparently and will do more than all the others put together to contribute to your overall life expectancy and health.

Of course you don't have to do any of this. You're a grown-up and can make your own decisions. But if you want to live long and prosper, it pays to think now.

> IF YOU WANT TO LIVE LONG AND PROSPER, IT PAYS TO THINK NOW

Be prepared for the pain and pleasure

Look, working for a living is always going to be a mixed bag. And the higher up you go, the more true this is. As a lowly accounts clerk, back when I first started out, I got used to being bored, idle, cheesed off, frustrated and sick of the job. By the time I had risen to being a general manager I was strangely surprised to find myself also bored, idle, cheesed off, frustrated and sick of the job.

But whereas when I was starting out I didn't expect any different, by the time I had risen to the heights I was totally unprepared for the same feelings. I guess I expected every day to be dramatic, exciting, utterly challenging, demanding, knife-edge stuff. And when it wasn't, I was, I guess, disappointed.

Now, of course, I realize that not every day can be fantastic. Some days will be boring. Some days will be adrenaline-filled and dramatic – but not as many as will be boring. You have to be prepared for the pain and the pleasure. You have to adjust your expectations so that you don't get cheesed off when it is boring, and don't explode with pleasure when it is too exciting for words.

YOU HAVE TO ADJUST YOUR EXPECTATIONS SO THAT YOU DON'T GET CHEESED OFF WHEN IT IS BORING

Trouble is, if it is boring, you might be tempted, as indeed I have been on many occasions, to liven it up a bit by being disruptive. Best sit on your hands and let the feeling pass. As a manager you aren't allowed to be disruptive – except in an innovative way of course.

RULE 61

Face the future

Whatever you are doing now, things are going to change. It is inevitable that the future will soon be upon us. Things will change, they have to. People you now work with will leave your team. Your sales figures will improve/slacken off. Your boss will retire/move on. Your customers will change. Your colleagues will be different. You, too, will change.

All these changes happen and it is the smart manager who not only embraces them but is prepared for them. Earlier we looked at having a Plan B and a Plan C; well, this is different – this is not catering for a specific crisis but being fluid and flexible enough to stay ahead of the game. What this means is that when change occurs you can take it in your stride and aren't thrown off course by it.

I once worked for a particular company that got taken over twice, in the space of a year. Each time the new people came in they had a whole series of changes to implement. They wanted things done 'their way'. This was fine, but after the first time we had barely got our breath back when the second takeover occurred.

I watched a lot of people fall by the wayside because they couldn't cope with the stress of having to stay so flexible. I was nearly one of them myself. It was a hard time but I saw then that resisting change was futile. Only by embracing the change could I survive – and not only survive but milk the situation to my advantage. The more I smiled and had a sort of 'bring it on' attitude the more responsibility I was given for the change itself. Other managers played the oak in the storm, but I was the willow. I bent and swayed and survived. They resisted, stood firm and lost branches.

You have to face your own future as well. Will you move on? Have you grown bored with the job, the industry, your role in it? What turns you on today may not in 10 years' time.

> RESISTING CHANGE
> WAS FUTILE. ONLY BY
> EMBRACING THE CHANGE
> COULD I SURVIVE

Head up, not head down

It's easy to adopt a head-down approach to life. It's harder to remain cheerful, head up. Is your glass half empty or half full? If it seems to be half empty, perhaps you need a holiday, a retraining schedule, a few new challenges, a new job, a new department, a new team – or simply a new approach. Life does tend to get fired at us at point-blank range and there is barely time to duck. The manager's lot is not always a happy or easy one and you get tired, despondent, bored, listless and just about ready to quit. We all do from time to time. Being a manager can feel like a thankless task. You get stuff shovelled at you from all directions. I'm never sure whether it's better to be at the top shovelling stuff downwards or at the bottom shovelling stuff upwards but I sure as hell know it's not great caught in the middle, fending it off from above and below.

Head up is both an affirmation (repeat it to yourself constantly when encountering problems, but silently, only to yourself, or they will section you) and a physical instruction – you can physically and emotionally (and probably mentally) practise head up.

While looking in a mirror, keep your head up and say, 'I feel really miserable'. You will laugh. Try the opposite. Head down, and say, 'I feel really happy'. Again you will find it impossible and silly.

> PHYSICALLY AND
> EMOTIONALLY (AND
> PROBABLY MENTALLY)
> PRACTISE HEAD UP

You will laugh. But you have to be looking in a mirror. Perhaps you always look like that. Either way it is funny. You are funny.

When entering a room it is head up. When chairing a meeting it is head up. When doing a presentation it is head up. When greeting people it is head up. When talking to staff it is head up. When talking to customers it is head up. At the end of a long and busy day, when you go to bed, you can do head down – and go to sleep knowing you've been big and bright and bold all day. Well done you.

RULE 63

See the wood *and* the trees

You've got to see the big picture. It's no good concentrating solely on what you do or what your department does. You can't even keep your gaze limited to what your organization does, or even what your industry does. You've got to see the wider view all the time. The good manager – that's you* – needs to have a good grasp of politics – both national and world – social history, world events, national intentions, international concerns, the environment, current legislation, proposed legislation** and technological developments (ones that may or may not affect your industry).

But you've also got to keep a close watch on what is going on under your nose – your team, your department, your immediate surroundings, the fine details as well as the big picture.

And how are you going to find the time to think about these things? To reflect, to analyze, to anticipate? You're going to schedule it into your diary, that's how. That's what proper grown-up managers do. And if you want to be a talented senior manager, you need to recognize the importance of giving yourself space to think. Sometimes you get the opportunity when you're travelling (but make sure you deliberately allocate the time, and use it wisely). Sometimes you have to block out an hour or two in the diary and make sure you're not disturbed. Call it 'planning time' if anyone asks – unless they're a successful manager themselves, in which case they'll understand.

---

* I keep saying, 'That's you'. You may wonder how I know. Because you are reading this. Bad managers think they know it all. You are prepared to read, to learn, to seek the advice of others, to widen your horizons, to have opinions, to stay abreast of current and new ideas and to keep an open mind by reading this far. That's good. You are good. Well done you.

** No, not just legislation that affects your industry but all big proposed legislation. You'd be surprised how often the 'knock-on' effect affects you.

The bright manager has to keep their eyes and ears open, their wits about them, their mind open to new ideas and innovations and trends. You've got to see the trees *and* the woods.

IT'S NO GOOD
CONCENTRATING SOLELY
ON WHAT YOU DO OR WHAT
YOUR DEPARTMENT DOES

Know when to let go

Sometimes it's really hard to let go, to know when to stop. But some projects just aren't going to work. Some team members are never going to fit in. Some bosses are never going to be possible to work with. Some situations must simply cease.

The good manager knows instinctively when to back off, to bail out, to retreat, to walk away whistling, pride intact and dignity in place. This Rule is for you but also for all the people who get caught, fool around, play up, try to defend the indefensible. Come on guys, know when to quit, know when the dog is dead.

A good manager knows when to hold their hands up: 'Yep, I messed up. It was my fault. I surrender.' Invariably you'll be forgiven because such an honest, direct approach throws 'em off the trail and they don't know how to handle you.

> ## KNOW WHEN TO QUIT,
> ## KNOW WHEN THE DOG
> ## IS DEAD

If you don't know when to let go you'll build up anger, resentment, stress, jealousy, pain. Learn to shrug and walk. You don't have to forgive or forget or anything, except drop it and walk away.

There is a myth in business that to get even is better than getting mad. But getting even is getting mad, it just takes a bit longer. Let it go. Concentrate on the next big exciting thing you can do.

Be decisive, even if it means being wrong sometimes

I bet you hate the type of manager who refuses to make a decent decision in case they make the wrong one. The prevaricating, indecisive, frightened manager who won't decide until it's too late or they get the decision made for them. I've worked for a few and there is nothing more irritating than someone who fence-sits because they don't know which way to jump – and all in the name of fear. They are frightened to decide in case they make a mistake – one that might cost them their job. Big deal. Better to jump and make a mistake than to sit there too frightened to make a move. Bring it on.

And suppose it does turn out to be the wrong decision. Well, sometimes out of big mistakes something bright and shiny and magical appears and we land on our feet with a tra-la and manage to look good despite sometimes not knowing what we were doing. This is the magic manager that I want you to be. The instinctive manager around whom anything can happen – and will. If you want to sit on a fence, go find another book to read.

Now I'm not saying here that you should make rash, ill-thought-through decisions. I'm assuming as a good manager that if it's that kind of decision, you have looked at the evidence before you and weighed it up, maybe asked for views from others. It's that point in the process I'm talking about – the point where you are tempted to shirk the decision, in case it turns out to be the wrong one.

This is about courage. The courage to be wrong sometimes. The courage to take a risk. The courage to be scared in a good way (sitting on a fence because you are scared is a lot different from taking a big decision and being scared but exhilarated).

All you've got to do is look at the facts, weigh them up, ask for advice, listen to your intuition and then do it – make the decision. Be dynamic, be bold.

> BETTER TO JUMP AND MAKE A
> MISTAKE THAN TO SIT THERE
> TOO FRIGHTENED TO
> MAKE A MOVE

Adopt minimalism as a management style

Minimalism means not issuing lengthy reports. It means not issuing memos every 20 minutes. It means keeping rules to the minimum* and letting people get on with their jobs. It means mission statements that make sense, are clear and easy to understand and are simple. It means management where managers use professionals and let them get on with their tasks in peace and quiet. It means managers who are secure in themselves and don't need to score points, bully or interfere.

Minimalist management is all about getting more by doing less. Yes, sure you have to be the boss, but it's more like steering a big ship – the tiniest touch of the wheel is enough. You swing that wheel violently from side to side and you're off course in an instant.

> **MINIMALIST MANAGEMENT**
> **IS ALL ABOUT GETTING**
> **MORE BY DOING LESS**

---

* No, not these Rules, I mean the petty ones – you have to wear a tie, you have to have one doughnut, not two, at coffee time, you have to address senior management as Mr/Mrs X and not use their first names, you have to park tidily, you have to wear sensible shoes, you have to . . . you know what I mean.

There is an old Chinese saying: 'Govern a country the same way you cook small fish', i.e. don't keep fiddling with them or they fall apart. Manage a department, team or company in pretty much the same way – gently, discreetly, unobtrusively. Better to be understated than too obvious.

RULE 67

Visualize your blue plaque

When you write your bestseller and then die you will get a blue plaque on the building where you were born, or lived, or wrote the damn thing – just so long as it was in London.* When I say 'you' I don't mean you, I mean whoever it is that lives there after you've snuffed it. This blue plaque is there to commemorate the fact that you did a good thing while you were alive. If you didn't do your good thing – i.e. write your bestseller, add to the sum of human literacy, manage to afford to live in London – you don't get a blue plaque.

Now imagine that there is a blue plaque for management style and it's not limited to London. What would you get yours for? Would you in fact get one? Basically, how would you like to be remembered? I worked for a boss once whose style of management was quaint to say the least. As he came in each day he would blast the first person he saw, give them a complete rollicking over whatever they happened to be doing. Then he would go to his office and have a coffee for half an hour. Then he would walk through the plant and compliment the first person he saw, tell them what a great job they were doing no matter what it was they were doing. I asked him about this and he said, 'Keeps them on their toes. They never know where they are with me. I get more out of them if they are frightened'. No blue plaque for you, Billy boy.

I've told this before because it still, after over 20 years, fascinates me as the worst incompetent, bullying stupidity I have ever come across. And he is still in a job, still employed by the same firm. Yes, he has hardly risen up the ranks, because he is still doing

---

* I'm fairly certain you have to be dead, but you don't have to have written anything. Being a musician is good enough – even Jimi Hendrix got one.

pretty much what he was then, back when I knew him, but he is still employed. I don't buy shares in that particular company – never have, never will.

I want a blue plaque. I want it for being the best damn manager there ever was. I want it for being good for my team, getting results, setting standards; for being a huge success and somebody they liked working for.

HOW WOULD YOU LIKE TO BE REMEMBERED?

RULE 68

Have principles and stick to them

When you think about it, you've got to have principles. If you don't, you end up despising yourself or in debt or in prison. You might end up like this anyway, but at least you could say, 'But I have my principles'.

There has to be a line beyond which you will not go. You have to know where that line is drawn. No one else has to know until they ask you to cross it and then you can tell them. That line has to be a 10-mile-high solid steel wall. You can't go beyond it, no matter what.

> THERE HAS TO BE A LINE
> BEYOND WHICH YOU WILL
> NOT GO. YOU HAVE TO
> KNOW WHERE THAT
> LINE IS DRAWN

I have a friend whose boss once asked her to falsify a formal warning letter to present at a tribunal for a member of staff who had been sacked and was claiming unfair dismissal. Would you do this? Does it matter whether you think the person was rightly or wrongly dismissed? Suppose they *had* been warned but it hadn't been recorded in writing? Suppose you and your boss were sure it must have been put in writing at the time, but you can't find it now? I'm not telling you what's right or wrong in this instance. I'm saying that *you* have to know what *you* consider to be right or wrong. And then stand by it.

So where would you draw your line? I've been asked to do things I didn't like. I've been asked to do things I found unpleasant. I've been asked to do things I found extremely irksome, but whenever I've been asked to cross my own personal line – which thankfully in a long business career has been only once or twice – I was able to say no, and stick to it. And each time I got a pat on the back rather than a trip to the Job Centre.

RULE 69

Follow your intuition

Deep down inside you know when you're right, and you know when you're wrong. Sure we can cut off that inner voice, but if we do we lose touch, and then we really are in trouble. That inner intuition may not speak loud and clear all the time but when it does you'd be mad not to follow it.

Trouble is, your mind also speaks loud and clear – all the time – and we mix the two up and follow what we think is intuition when in fact it is fear or jealousy or another emotion.

So how do you tell? If when you're talking to somebody about a new system you are about to implement and, though they look positive, you feel an odd or cold feeling inside, heed it. Take time to think why. Tell somebody else about it and see if it happens again. Go back to the plan and look at it from all viewpoints, considering all the stakeholders. Are you still convinced?

Never be too proud or too lazy to get more feedback, to find a sounding board or to rethink a proposal or a decision if you've got a bad feeling about it.

Look at previous good or bad decisions you've made. How did you feel about them at the time? Did you, deep down, know a bad course of action was flawed before you followed it? Would you know that feeling again?

Developing your intuition is a hard thing to teach, but if you make a habit of 'listening' to how you feel about something, your radar will improve and you'll begin to know when a gut feeling is telling you that something isn't right.

IF YOU MAKE A HABIT OF 'LISTENING' TO HOW YOU FEEL ABOUT SOMETHING, YOUR RADAR WILL IMPROVE

Be creative

The good manager keeps a store cupboard full of creative techniques so that when they get stuck, when the team gets stuck – and you and they will from time to time – you have something to fall back on.

Being creative is about finding new and different ways to solve problems. You get stuck and start worrying and then you go off and tend your garden, do some washing up, fly a kite or whatever, and you get immersed in what you are doing and answers bubble up to the surface.

Most creative techniques get you to switch off your conscious, thinking brain and start to use a deeper, more intuitive part of your mind. And that part has a whole load of answers that we can't normally access. This is the part we can access during sleep or meditation or by using creative thinking techniques.

> GET IMMERSED IN WHAT
> YOU ARE DOING AND
> ANSWERS BUBBLE UP TO
> THE SURFACE

Watch what other managers do – the ones you admire and respect. They probably have a store cupboard of creative tricks. Pinch a few. Read up on creative thinking techniques. Find out what the bright managers are doing, thinking, trying out. Ask somebody not in your field what they would do. Don't be afraid to be wacky or off the wall – after all, some of the best ideas have come from dreams.

RULE 71

Don't stagnate

So are you a leader or a manager? Not really a fair question when we've spent the whole book so far making sure you are an effective, efficient and startlingly good manager. But the really good managers are also leaders – they inspire and motivate, encourage and enthuse. They draw people to them like moths to a flame. They are charismatic and dynamic and stylish. They are leaders indeed.

But they are also good managers. Too much management and you stagnate. You have to revel in change, seek new challenges, stay on your toes, find new ways of doing things, motivate your team in new and exciting ways, introduce new technology and ideas, start trends, jump fences, light fires. You can't be seen to stand still or moss will grow over you and you become a fixture and people stop noticing you.

> THE REALLY GOOD
> MANAGERS ARE ALSO
> LEADERS – THEY INSPIRE
> AND MOTIVATE,
> ENCOURAGE AND ENTHUSE

I know it's difficult sometimes to see beyond today's workload, tomorrow's meetings, next week's directors' report. But you have to be moving or you will stagnate. Set aside a little time each day or week – only half an hour perhaps – to think up new ways of being revolutionary. Why? Because if you don't do this you become bogged down in the day-to-day, the humdrum, the routine. Yes, you are a manager, but you are also an innovator, motivator, inspirer, leader, trendsetter.

If the moss has already grown over you and people have come to regard you as part of the furniture you will have to work very hard to shake off that image. Don't scare them with radical change – do it bit by bit.

RULE 72

Be flexible and ready to move on

There will come a time when it's time to move on. Other jobs are waiting to be done. Other teams are waiting to be led. You may have to pack up camp and hit the trail. So keep your eyes open for opportunities. As Thomas Edison once said, 'Opportunity is missed by most people because it comes dressed in overalls and looks like work'.

Remember your long-term plan – and I bet it didn't include stuff like, 'Stay here until I retire and/or turn to dust' – and keep looking to distant horizons.

Being a good manager, a fantastic manager, often means you get sought out, head-hunted, poached. Be ready to be enticed away. Doesn't mean you have to go, but be open to offers – how flattering.

Stay on your toes and be ready to move sideways; be prepared to look at unusual opportunities. Be ready perhaps to go it alone if that's in your long-term plan.

> **BE READY TO MOVE**
> **SIDEWAYS; BE PREPARED**
> **TO LOOK AT UNUSUAL**
> **OPPORTUNITIES**

Should you feel guilty at abandoning your team? No. You have a career and that involves moving on. Your team may benefit from a breath of fresh air coming in after you to blow the cobwebs away. I've left managerial jobs where the staff seemed genuinely surprised that I would dare to leave, to spread my wings and go 'elsewhere', as if it was a dark and dangerous country that would gobble me up. Of course, once I had left I gained a reputation as a 'deserter' for leaving, but better that than 'good riddance'.

RULE 73

Remember the object of the exercise

My fellow writer Carmel McConnell says in *Get Ahead; Give a Damn:* 'Happy, fulfilled, stretched but supported people generally achieve the most at work and get the most from life. They drain a lot of swamps – and have a pretty good time doing it (strange though it may seem swamp drainage is a Very Enjoyable Occupation). However, many of us face a few alligators . . . those subversive obstacles that get in the way of a productive, high achieving but low-stress kind of life. Some of them we make ourselves, some of them are placed there by other people. Some of them just are.'

And the object of the exercise, my friend, is what? We all have a different agenda. You may say, 'To make profits for the shareholders' (Rule 52), but you're just trying to curry favour by giving an answer you think I want. I don't.

Remember that even when you are up to your arse in alligators the object of the exercise was to drain the swamp. There are many objectives, many swamp-draining exercises. You might see it as the next project, setting the next budget, getting through the next interview, week or disciplinary interview. It might be long-term stuff, career in general, etc. And the alligators who bite your bum could be colleagues, customers, clients, bosses, staff, family, you name it/them. But they do get in the way of draining the swamp.

This is a Rule about focusing so you don't get side-tracked by all the nonsense that goes on around you. Stay focused and keep the objective in your sights at all times – whatever it may be.

STAY FOCUSED AND KEEP THE
OBJECTIVE IN YOUR SIGHTS
AT ALL TIMES – WHATEVER
IT MAY BE

RULE 74

Remember that none of us has to be here

I once worked with a fabulous manager. Sadly he is no longer with us but I remember all the managerial stuff he taught me. He was one of us – seemingly. On the surface he played the company game, discreet, charming, efficient, hard-working, but deep down this man worked for no one but himself.

Bob was an individualist, a rule breaker (but not these Rules – most of these came from him), non-conformist, maverick. He trod a fine line. He was Mr Cool Dude. Mr Management Should Never Be Seen To Be Done.

Sure, he got the job done and done extremely well, but he was a managerial rebel. He and I were scheduled once to go on a manager's training course. Guess who failed to show up? Yep, Bob. He wasn't going to make LEGO models for anyone.

I went. I made LEGO models. I toed the company line. Guess who got promoted? Yep, right again. Bob.

So how did we get here? Ah, moaning. I moaned. Bob would say, 'None of us has to be here'. And he meant it. Literally. Literally none of us has to be here. We don't have to do the job. We can walk any time we want. This means we are here by choice. We have chosen to be here. We choose to be here each and every day. It is our choice. If we have chosen to be here then surely it means we are enjoying it – or we wouldn't be here? Right? If we aren't enjoying it then we should choose not to be here.

Basically what Bob was saying to me was, 'Stop moaning – enjoy it or leave'. This doesn't mean you can't point out the things that are wrong, but if they aren't going to get solved you'd better learn to live with them. Enjoy it or move over and let someone else do the job who will. None of us has to be here.

STOP MOANING – ENJOY IT OR LEAVE

RULE 75

Go home

Another manager I worked with stayed late, got in early, skipped lunch and kept his head down and grafted every second he was there. Guess who got promoted over him? Yep, Bob again from Rule 74. Mr Cool Dude.

One of Bob's favourite lines, to me anyway, was, 'Go home, Rich, go home. You've got a young family, go home and see them before they forget what you look like. Either that or send them a photo before they really forget'. Naturally I went home. As did Bob, a lot. In fact he was at work so little he got promoted again.

His secret? His team, of which I was one, would have done anything for him. We went that extra mile. We would never have willingly let him down. Bob inspired loyalty in his staff in a way I've rarely seen since. He made all of us feel grown-up, trusted, treated in a respectful way. He never shouted, abused, put upon, demanded, overworked, or humiliated his team. I never saw him have to discipline anyone, ever. He was charismatic and charming, cool and relaxed. He cooked us all like small fish.

He said his secret was his family. For them he worked. He adored his children and would rather have been home with them than working. His love for them showed and he wore the badge of happy family man with great pride. He talked a lot about his kids and his wife and was obviously very happy with them.

He never stayed late because that would have been disloyal to his number-one priority – his family. This gave him great depth. He was well rounded and balanced. He was at ease with himself. He had nothing to prove at work because he was content at home. I've worked with some complete bastards and I can say the only thing they all had in common was a bad home life. Their base camp was corrupt and it showed. So, my dear friend, go home.

> HE HAD NOTHING TO PROVE
> AT WORK BECAUSE HE WAS
> CONTENT AT HOME

Keep learning – especially from the opposition

We've all heard the manager who gets angry when the competition steals a march on them. Or who rails about how unfair it was that they lost such and such an order. Or when a client goes off them, screams blue murder that they've been stitched up. Wrong, wrong, wrong. Believe me, if the competition is stealing your ideas, your customers, your contracts, your clients, your sales, your staff and your income, then you have (a) no one to blame but yourself, and (b) been given a great opportunity to learn how to do it better.

Nothing teaches us better than a better competitor. What is it they are doing? What can we learn from this? How can we emulate them? How can we take what they are doing and really run with it? How can we grow our market share by outdoing what they are doing?

Spend some time each week checking what the competition is doing, because if they are effective (and competition invariably is) they will be checking out what you are doing. Spend some time getting to know – and sharing with – the competition. Look, if you have five main competitors and you share with them, you are giving each one a part of what you are doing. But the idea spreads and *five* will give you ideas, information, research, etc. We should never fear competition. Embrace it. It grows the market. It keeps you on your toes. It gives you a real learning opportunity – real as in it is actually happening and isn't a training exercise. And it doesn't involve LEGO.

If you fear competition, what you really fear is your own incompetence. If you know you're doing a good job the competition can't touch you. If you're not doing a good job the competition can walk all over you – and you know it, just as you know you're not doing a good job.

> **IF YOU FEAR COMPETITION,**
>
> **WHAT YOU REALLY FEAR IS**
>
> **YOUR OWN INCOMPETENCE**

RULE 77

Be passionate and bold

If you're not going to be passionate about your work what are you going to be passionate about? Look, you spend more time at work doing work, living, breathing and being work, than anything else except perhaps sleeping. You must be passionate about what you do. You're passionate about sex, but that doesn't last as long as your career. You're passionate about food and you only eat three times a day – work is continual. You're passionate about your life, your hobbies, your family, your holidays. And yet an awful lot of people see their work as something to dread, a chore to be got through. If it's like that for you, then go home – and stay there. Make room for someone who is going to be passionate about it. But I'm positive that isn't you.

When I first started my career – of which I have had several – I read up on the industry before I started training. I read about its history, the famous people in it, stories about it, how it evolved and the legislation surrounding it, how certain traditions associated with it came about. I went into that job a walking encyclopaedia of facts and information, anecdotes and history. And I had my breath taken away by how little everyone else in that industry knew. I was passionate and it seemed no one else was. I found only a terribly small group of people who cared about what they did. Over the years I have met many others, but never enough.

Once you are passionate you can be bold, because you have that drive, that enthusiasm, that courage, that excitement. Being bold means you can take risks. And taking risks means they pay off – not all the time but often enough that you get a name for yourself as a high-flyer, a go-getter, a success.

Being passionate means caring about what you do. Not just going through the motions but really caring. Being driven – being constantly excited and enthusiastic. What you do makes a difference

– it's not just about the money or the status or the perks. It's about making a real contribution to people's lives and the environment and society. If you're not passionate, what are you? If you are passionate, what are you passionate about? If not now, when?

> ONCE YOU ARE PASSIONATE
> YOU CAN BE BOLD, BECAUSE
> YOU HAVE THAT DRIVE,
> THAT ENTHUSIASM, THAT
> COURAGE, THAT EXCITEMENT

RULE 78

Plan for the worst, but hope for the best

As a manager, you should prepare for the worst and hope for the best. What's your worst-case scenario? All the staff phone in sick because it's World Cup Final? You lose that big order? Sales slump to zero? Building burns down? National strikes? Flu epidemic? Terrorist attack? Oil spillage? Health and Safety close you down? All or any of these things can play havoc with your budget figures.

So what contingency plans do you have in place in case this worst-case scenario actually happens? Huh? Yep, thought so. You've got to have emergency plans, panic routes mapped out, procedures for crisis management, actions wrapped up and in the bag, replacement crews sorted, alternative sources of income laid down. You have to have a plan.

Now chances are you won't ever have to implement this plan. With luck and divine intervention it will always remain a plan – nothing more. But a plan you have to have.

Now, you are allowed to hope. Hope it ain't never gonna happen. Hope the sun will forever shine. I was once asked by a special committee what I would do in the event of a major bomb scare at the company where I worked. My answer, 'Hope it's a hoax', made them laugh but earned me no brownie points at all. 'What about a plan?' I was asked. 'Oh, I've got one of those as well', I said and I may have recovered about half a point. Have a plan – and a lot of hope.

HAVE A PLAN – AND
A LOT OF HOPE

RULE 79

Let the company see you are on its side

To let the company see you are on its side you need to do some concrete things. Such as:

- buy some shares
- read the company newsletter – better still, edit the damn thing
- support company functions
- show an interest
- ask questions
- have your interest in the company noticed and recorded in some way
- focus on what you contribute to the company, not on what you get out of it
- use the company's products or services
- actively speak well of the company
- rehearse saying what you think is good about the company – have a ready answer to hand if asked
- know the company's mission statement and philosophy
- know the company's products and/or services inside and out
- know the company history – its formation, its mergers and acquisitions, etc., its long-term goals and its key personnel (founder, etc.)
- know the company's social standing and what it does for the community.

What you do not do – *ever* – is bad-mouth the company, under any circumstances.

'But, but, but', I hear you say, 'Won't this make me out to be an oik, a toady, a yes-person, a lackey, a company mouthpiece?' Nope. Not if you do it right. If you mouth platitudes and seem insincere people will know it is an act and that you are a company pawn. But if you are strong about it people will take your lead and follow suit. Set an example. Be outspoken in your praise for the company. It is such an unfashionable thing to do you will make your mark, but you do have to be sincere and bold.

'But what if I don't feel so good about the company?' Then get out. It's a two-way process. They employ you. You work for them. You give and they give. You take and they take. If you're unhappy about this relationship, then get out, get a divorce, find another lover. You have to love your company and see it as a relationship. If you're in a bad one, what are you going to do about it? Put up and shut up? I do hope not.

> # SET AN EXAMPLE. BE OUTSPOKEN IN YOUR PRAISE FOR THE COMPANY

Don't bad-mouth your boss

OK, so your boss is a jerk and you can't stand working under such a weasel and you've just got to tell everyone you meet what a fool this boss is. Yes? No. Wrong, wrong, wrong. You do not bad-mouth your boss under any circumstances. OK, so your whole team knows your boss is useless and they make that clear to you. Do you agree? No, you do not. Never, ever. If you can't find anything good to say, then say nothing at all. You do not slag them off even if they deserve it, or you feel they do anyway.

Your boss is your boss. If they are that dreadful then don't work for them, go look someplace else. If you are going to work for them then that is your choice and you have to stick with it, live with it, support it, believe in it – or you'll go mad.

If your boss is a nightmare it is your job to turn that around. Get them to trust you. Then get them to delegate to you. Then get them to hand over responsibility to you. Then replace them. Simple, isn't it? Obviously not, but these are the steps you must take if you are serious and committed.

Watch what you say about your boss in case it gets back to their own boss – who might just happen to be a fan of your boss and not take kindly to you bad-mouthing them. After all, they put them there and for you to question that decision publicly leaves you in a precarious situation yourself.

I once worked for a complete son of a . . . who drank, kept bad company and didn't know if it was New York or New Year most of the time. Someone complained about him to head office and a deputation was sent down to take statements. Twelve junior managers, including myself, were questioned about his behaviour. I refused to co-operate and said nothing. A year later my boss was still there and I was still there but 11 other junior managers no longer worked for that company. Moral: keep schtum if you can't be nice. How come he survived? Beats me. He obviously had juice in the right places. How did I survive? No idea. He trusted me and I kept my head down and got on with my job; his behaviour didn't affect me unduly and I coped.

> # IF YOU CAN'T FIND ANYTHING GOOD TO SAY, THEN SAY NOTHING AT ALL

Don't bad-mouth your team

So you can't bad-mouth the company and you can't slag off your boss. 'Surely', I hear you ask, 'I can criticize my team?' Not in public you can't. Behind closed doors when there is no one there but you and you alone, then and only then are you allowed one small silent scream when things really hit the fan, but apart from that, nothing.

It's a poor work person who blames their tools. Your team is your tool to getting your management job done. If your team is useless it is you who hasn't sharpened the tool, oiled it, cleaned the rust off, repaired the handle, replaced worn-out bits, checked for damage, that sort of thing.

Your team will make mistakes, that's a given. Things will go wrong, that too is a given. You're dealing with people; they screw up from time to time, get emotional, let you down, fail to work as a team, goof off and generally behave completely normally. You'd be a fool not to expect this, to plan for it, to build it into your plans. Look, things go wrong and slagging off your team doesn't help. Learn from it and move on.

> THINGS GO WRONG AND
> SLAGGING OFF YOUR TEAM
> DOESN'T HELP. LEARN FROM
> IT AND MOVE ON

You have to 'publicly celebrate those who move the organization closer to the attainment of its vision and strategic goal' – that's your team, that is. If you slag your team off you are focusing on the negative, which will spiral them downwards. If you praise them it's an uplifting experience.

If you slag your team off you are slagging yourself off and admitting publicly you are a crap manager. Don't do it – you're not.

Accept that some things bosses tell you to do will be wrong

Just because you do your job well doesn't mean everyone else does. Some bosses are useless and there's no getting away from that. Sometimes they will tell you to do stuff that is crazy. Sometimes they will issue orders that are so obviously off the wall you can't help but gasp. Sometimes they will tell you to do things that are completely wrong. What are you to do?

You have various options:

- refuse

- leave

- seek advice from your union/management advisory body/ trade body if you are in one

- ask advice from Human Resources

- ask advice from other managers

- ask advice from your boss's boss

- put your concerns in writing

- get on and do it but grumble a lot

- get on and do it with a cheerful smile and a whistle

- talk to your boss about your misgivings.

Initially it might be politic to go and talk to your boss in person, face-to-face, over an informal coffee; a bit of a chat, nothing too heavy. Point out you think you have a problem with their order. Don't make it personal. Don't attack them. Don't tell them they are crap. Explain that it is you that has the problem. The order and your boss are fine but you feel uncomfortable. Put the ball firmly back in their lap. If they insist, end by saying you still feel uncomfortable about it and would like time to seek further advice. Ask if you can put your fears in writing and whether they would do the same.

Sometimes you have to accept that bosses don't know what they are doing, ain't going to change and you have to put up with it. Or you could simply refuse or leave. Your call. The Rule is that you should accept it happens from time to time.

> # SOMETIMES YOU HAVE TO ACCEPT THAT BOSSES DON'T KNOW WHAT THEY ARE DOING

RULE 83

Accept that bosses are as scared as you are at times

Poor loves, they too get frightened, paranoid, lost, feel unloved, confused, at sea, vulnerable and alone. Your job is to take away your bosses' pain, their fears and make them relax.

You are a manager and have to manage not only downwards but upwards as well. When you deal with your bosses you mustn't ever:

- threaten
- usurp
- intimidate
- pressurize
- menace
- disrespect
- question (apart from under Rule 82)
- undermine
- ridicule.

Instead you have to support, back, encourage, comfort, console, cheer up, relieve the pressure on, be utterly dependable, take the strain, guard the fort and eventually perhaps replace them – with yourself of course.

Some bosses are so stricken with panic they are incapable of making decisions. You will have to make decisions for them and reassure them that everything is fine – Nurse is here now and they can go and lie down.

> ## YOUR JOB IS TO TAKE AWAY YOUR BOSSES' PAIN, THEIR FEARS AND MAKE THEM RELAX

RULE 84

Avoid straitjacket thinking

When you've got your head down and things are flying at you from all directions, it is easy to forget that you are supposed to be an innovative, creative, cutting-edge sort of manager. We all do it. We get so close to the work under our noses we lose sight of the fact that we *can* invent, inspire, lead, motivate – and say yes. The team comes to you with a new idea and you are so weary from fighting the bureaucracy, the system, the weather and the commuting that you just say no, no matter what it is they are suggesting. It's often a no with a subtext of 'And leave me alone, I'm too busy/stressed/irritable to think about this now'. Is that you? Bet it is sometimes. It's all of us.

So, we need to throw the straitjacket off. We need to lift our heads. We need to consider the options and think 'Why not?' and 'What *would* happen if we did this?' We need to stop being constrained by pressure and by work.

> IT IS EASY TO FORGET THAT YOU ARE SUPPOSED TO BE AN INNOVATIVE, CREATIVE, CUTTING-EDGE SORT OF MANAGER

An easy way out of the straitjacket is to consider how you would view your job, your department, your team if you were a stranger coming in from the outside, coming in to do your job for the very first time. What would you change? What would you leave alone? Think of what you're doing from the point of view of your customers – what makes sense? What doesn't?

It is terribly easy to get so bogged down in minutiae that we fail to stand back and look at things with fresh eyes every day. But if we are to be simply the best sort of manager ever to roam the Earth, we must stay fresh or go the way of the dinosaurs. Staying fresh means being open to new ideas, new suggestions, new concepts and new directions.

Act and talk as if one of *them*

OK, before you actually *become* one of them, you should be *practising* to become one of them. If you are a junior manager you should be studying the way middle managers walk and talk and be ready to become one. If you are a middle manager you should be acting and talking as if you were already a senior manager. And on, right up to the top.

When I first became a managing director of a company, I almost forgot this Rule. I carried on managing as if I was a senior manager. But sales weren't going as well as I would have liked. I was organizing corporate sales and couldn't get to talk to the right people. I read somewhere that kings only talk to kings. I became a king (substitute 'managing director' for 'king' and you'll see what I mean). Immediately doors which previously had been closed were opened and sales exceeded my expectations.

> IF YOU ARE A MIDDLE
> MANAGER YOU SHOULD
> BE ACTING AND TALKING
> AS IF YOU WERE ALREADY
> A SENIOR MANAGER

If you're going to be a king in the future you had better start practising now. Watch how anyone senior to you does things. The way
they answer the phone, talk to staff, what they wear, what paper
they read, how they get to work, what they do at work and how
they do it.

I recently met a managing director of a very large company and I
was seriously impressed with how friendly and informal he was
with his staff – who obviously adored him – and how genuinely
relaxed he seemed. That is until we came to negotiate, when he
was obviously totally up on his job and had facts and figures at
his fingertips in a second. I watched him because he is my next
step, if you like. He is my 'one of them'.

And no, no matter how high you go, you never walk on people – ever.

RULE 86

If in doubt, ask questions

Why don't we ask questions more? Are we worried that people will think we don't know enough already? The smartest operators are those who do ask questions, all the time, and they invariably benefit from doing so. It's not so much a specific strategy for a particular purpose, as a general approach that can be helpful in all kinds of ways.

For a start you'll learn a lot more about your team if you ask them more questions: 'Why do you think we're going about it in the wrong way?' 'What do you think is slowing up the invoicing process?' 'How would you tackle this customer?' And you may elicit solutions you wouldn't have done otherwise. And encourage them to express opinions or offer suggestions or submit ideas.

Asking questions is also a classic solution when you're in a tight corner. If you don't believe me, just listen to politicians being interviewed by pushy journalists. It's a standard response. When your boss asks you to explain something tricky, respond with, 'Why do you think that?' or 'Is this something our customers have been saying to you?' At the least it will buy you a little time, and at best it may provide you with usable information.

Questions are a top way to tell people they're being absurd without telling them they're being absurd. It's especially helpful therefore when dealing with inept bosses. Instead of saying, 'That will never work' or something similarly inflammatory (if heartfelt), you just ask, 'What outcome are you hoping for from this?' or 'How do you think the design team will cope with that?' or 'In what way will that improve our performance?' or 'What effect do you expect that to have on sales?'

So long as you adopt a tone of friendly enquiry, it's very hard to cause offence with a question. However, it's a very effective way to draw attention to the flaw in any plan, and to get other people to damn themselves without you having made any accusation at all.

It makes sense to ask questions about any new proposal of course, and generally people will. What's rarer is a manager who keeps on asking questions, even difficult ones, throughout a project to ensure that nothing is overlooked. But that's the kind of manager you're going to be from now on. Far too many people get the proposal accepted or the project launched, and then sit back and let it run. If it hits problems, they deal with it. But if you keep asking questions, there's a far better chance you'll spot the problems before you hit them.

> # SO LONG AS YOU ADOPT A TONE OF FRIENDLY ENQUIRY, IT'S VERY HARD TO CAUSE OFFENCE WITH A QUESTION

Show you understand the viewpoint of underlings *and* overlings

Being an underling – as we all know because we've all done it, been there – is tough. You get to take a lot of orders from a lot of people delivered in a way that puts your back up and makes you angry.

But hey, being a manager is often no better. Now you are caught in the middle. You get all that flak from the staff, plus all the crazy directives from the chief executive. You are no longer an underling and not quite an overling. You are the middle of the sandwich. You're going to get it from both directions, upwards and downwards.

One of the best ways to take the pressure off is to let them all know you understand their viewpoint. Don't just smile and say, 'Yeah, I know where you're coming from', when it is plainly obvious you don't. You really have to make sure they know you do understand their needs and wants, grievances and demands, fears and hopes. Up and down the chain.

When push comes to shove you are going to have to side with the overlings sometimes. When you think they are right of course. Your underlings – non-PC for team – will obviously resent this, particularly as they will not welcome any changes (especially ones they don't understand). This is a good time to let them tell you how they feel and tell them that you do understand this, and explain why the overlings have decided to do what they have.

If you're really good, one day you'll learn to explain how the underlings perceive things to the overlings, in terms they will understand – and vice versa. If you can get the underlings to see why the overlings believe that something not in their best interests makes sense, then you're on the road to becoming a managerial genius.

> ONE OF THE BEST WAYS
> TO TAKE THE PRESSURE
> OFF IS TO LET THEM ALL
> KNOW YOU UNDERSTAND
> THEIR VIEWPOINT

RULE 88

Add value

Many years ago I saw Robin Day presenting an episode of *Question Time* and he asked one of the panel a question. The panellist replied, 'All I can really do is repeat what I said earlier . . . ', at which point Robin Day cut him off abruptly, saying, 'Well, let's not bother with that then', and turned to another panellist, leaving the first one stunned.

I was hugely impressed with both Day's comic timing and – more importantly – the sentiment. Why bother to speak if you have nothing to add? And yet people do, all the time. They repeat what they said before. They rephrase earlier contributions. They say things that are completely meaningless. Why? How do they think this is helping? And why do they think they were asked to contribute if they have nothing useful to say?

Listen, if you want to be well respected, you should have listened to what was being said, read the information you were given, researched the background, thought about the issue – and formed an opinion that you can back up. On top of that, you should have come up with creative solutions, inventive suggestions, original approaches, constructive ideas. Are you trying to impress people or aren't you?

You might find it instructive to listen to what other people say in meetings and secretly grade them on a scale of 1–10 according to how useful they are to the discussion. It will tell you a lot about your fellow managers, and you should find that the high scorers among them are also the high flyers.

The people who have nothing to contribute but find something pointless to say anyway are not simply failing to help. They are actively wasting everyone's time. I've sat through meetings where if you cut out all the time-wasting waffle from people with nothing better to say, you could slash hours off the duration of the meeting. This is not Rules behaviour, and don't ever catch yourself doing it. You must be the one to set the standard – regardless of whether other people rise to it or not. And you can be sure that while some of your colleagues may not seem to notice, your own managers will be well aware that you're someone to listen to, because your contributions add value.

And what if you really have nothing helpful to say, or you've already contributed your thoughts and are asked again for your input? Well, in that case, decline to comment. Politely say that you have nothing – or nothing, further – to add.

> YOU MUST BE THE ONE
> TO SET THE STANDARD –
> REGARDLESS OF WHETHER
> OTHER PEOPLE RISE TO
> IT OR NOT

Don't back down – be prepared to stand your ground

There will be times when you are certain and know you're right. In these times sometimes you have to make a stand. You have to be prepared to put up or shut up. You have to be prepared to fight for what you believe in. If you are passionate about what you do, then standing up for what you know is right isn't that hard.

You don't have to be aggressive, just resolute. If you are being bullied, say so loud and clear – chances are the person harassing you will back off, quick.

You don't have to be rude, just assertive. If someone is spreading rumours about you or your team or your performance that aren't true, then collar them. State your position clearly: 'I hear you are spreading such and such a rumour. This is not true and I would appreciate it if you would stop.'

You don't have to be angry, just be very certain of yourself and very well prepared. If someone always finds fault with what you suggest, such as 'Oh, that won't work, we tried it before and it failed', then stand your ground and don't back down. Say, 'Yes, and here are the figures to show why it didn't work. And here is my report to explain why it will work this time and how it is different'.

You don't have to get fired, just fired up. If you work for a boss who fails to give you suitable feedback, keep plugging away. Ask, 'How can I improve my performance for next time? What steps should I take to get that pay rise I want that you've just said no to? Where do you see me in a year's time? What can we do to improve sales?' Keep pushing the ball back into their court until they are forced to give you suitable answers.

You don't have to be argumentative, just conciliatory. If you have a boss suggesting you cut legal corners, don't point-blank refuse and cause an argument. Instead say, 'Ah. How would we handle this if the media/auditors got hold of it?' You aren't refusing but you are standing your ground and not going along with their ideas – and you are also offering them a way out. They won't have to make a point and impose their will on you, but they can now diplomatically back down without losing face.

> IF YOU ARE PASSIONATE ABOUT WHAT YOU DO, THEN STANDING UP FOR WHAT YOU KNOW IS RIGHT ISN'T THAT HARD

RULE 90

Don't play politics

Politicians are people paid to play politics. You are not. You are a manager. You manage situations and projects. The people don't need managing. They manage themselves. Some of them go off the rails sometimes and play politics. You don't have to play with them. That's like playing on the rails. You're bound to get hurt, bound to get run over by a train. Playing politics is using people to further your own ends, which, if you are playing politics properly, will be unpleasant, selfish, narrow-minded and petty. Playing politics invariably involves intimidating people, being sly, getting things done by lying or other dishonest means, not being yourself or true to others and generally behaving appallingly. There, I've said it now and I guess you know what I think of playing politics – it stinks.

You should 'love thy neighbour, but pick thy neighbourhood'. Try to hang out with OK-people who don't feel the need to play politics.

Try to be involved with less popular projects because they attract less attention, less competition. Same goes for the less popular team or department. Here you can shine without having to compete all the time. Every company has people who get stuff done without backstabbing. Hang out with these people.

Share information, always. This takes the wind out of the sails of those who do play politics. Be everyone's friend so no one can accuse you of being cliquey or stand-offish.

Although you aren't going to play, you still have to be on your guard – be aware that playing politics goes on and be ready to deal with it in an appropriate way. Watch out for the hidden agendas that go on, the concealing true motives, the smear campaigns, the lying, the gossip (often malicious), the hints and subtle nuances that you aren't up to scratch or speed, the jockeying for power and control, the whispering, that sort of thing. If you are fortunate you will encounter very little of it and any you do can be cut off sharpish. Some industries seem to breed that sort of bad behaviour and you will be hard pushed to stop it. Refuse to play, and get a reputation for being a straight-talking, unpolitical being – honest, above board, open, candid, guileless and straightforward. Nothing complicated about you.

EVERY COMPANY HAS PEOPLE
WHO GET STUFF DONE
WITHOUT BACK-STABBING.
HANG OUT WITH
THESE PEOPLE

Don't slag off other managers

Earlier we looked at how competition should spur you on, encourage you, and how you should never be frightened of it. We were talking about the competition of other industries, other organizations.

But what of colleagues and other departments? Same goes. Don't be frightened of anyone or anything. If you are good at what you do, bold, creative, fast on your feet – as I am sure you are – then there is no need. If you refuse to engage in politics then you will be seen as honest and trustworthy. You should never criticize, make inferences about, slag off, condemn, pass judgement on or whinge about your colleagues or people from other departments/divisions.

> IF YOU REFUSE TO ENGAGE
> IN POLITICS THEN YOU WILL
> BE SEEN AS HONEST AND
> TRUSTWORTHY

If you do, you will be seen as weak or a poor performer. Sure, others will, and will be seen to profit from it at times. But do they sleep at night? Can they, hand on heart, swear they enjoy their job, or do they fear others stitching them up as they have stitched up others? I think not. I've worked with quite a few. They harp on about how good they are, how bad everyone else is, but they quake in their boots privately because deep down they know they aren't as good at their jobs as those whom they criticize.

Just because someone points out your faults doesn't make you any less of an emperor, does it? And if you see another emperor with their new clothes there is no point in pointing it out to them that they have been fooled – no one will thank you.

I worked with one manager who would bang on incessantly about all the other managers and how bad they were. Interesting thing was every fault he pointed out, he was equally guilty of. We laughed because it was so obvious to everyone but him. He couldn't see he was highlighting his own faults.

Share what you know

This Rule is about mentoring people who know less than you. They don't have to know that much less and you don't have to know that much more. But if you share everything you do know then they will know as much as you.

Some managers will see this as a threat. They are the foolish ones. What you have just done is train up someone to take some of the workload from your shoulders. Someone to replace you when you get promoted.

Some managers feel awkward about sharing because they feel they don't know enough. But when you learnt English at school it was enough that your teacher knew about grammar and clauses and punctuation and that sort of stuff. You didn't need an award-winning novelist or a Nobel prize winner. No, just a humble English teacher was enough.

> ## SOME MANAGERS WILL SEE THIS AS A THREAT. THEY ARE THE FOOLISH ONES

And what are you going to share with your team? That's easy. Anything that might help them do their job better: information, tactics, plans, skills, ideas, reading material, contacts, lunch – just keep giving them all the tools you can to make them more useful to you and to themselves.

Sharing with colleagues is important too. The more you give out the more you'll get back. Suppose you give one bit of information to 20 other managers. If only half of them are generous enough to return the favour it means you now have ten bits of new information to add to your collection. They have only gained by one but you have gained by ten – brilliantly easy. They will invariably share with you, but not each other – don't ask me why. Perhaps they feel indebted to you and not to them.

RULE 93

Don't intimidate

Being a manager gives you authority and power, no doubt about that. Perhaps that's what separates good managers like you from rubbish ones. You know how to handle that power and you don't abuse it.

People will look up to you as a manager, respect you and even fear you. You have the power of unemployment or work over them and they will be aware of that in all their dealings with you. But you have to try and overcome that by getting them to trust you. Always be predictable so that they know where they are with you at all times and you don't frighten them by taking them unawares. You mustn't abuse your position by intimidating your team.

Yes, there are two ways of getting things done – fear and reward – and a lot of managers choose the first because they feel under-confident, unsure and uncertain. Unlike you they aren't at ease with themselves and this shows up in a threatening or bullying attitude towards their staff. We ought to pity them – or, if we work under such a boss ourselves, try and get them better trained. Perhaps leave a copy of this book lying around for them to stumble on accidentally?

A lot of managers don't know that their attitude sets the standard for how their staff treat each other and their customers. If they see a manager who is kind and co-operative, rewarding to work for and confident, it rubs off and they, in turn, act the same way towards each other and towards customers as well.

Working this way makes life easier and more productive. It's so much better to work in an organization where reward is used instead of fear to get things done.

IT'S SO MUCH BETTER TO
WORK IN AN ORGANIZATION
WHERE REWARD IS USED
INSTEAD OF FEAR TO GET
THINGS DONE

RULE 94

Be above interdepartmental warfare

I once worked for two bosses at the same time. They were two directors of the company and they hated each other. Each had an agenda. Each fought a vicious campaign against the other with us managers – and staff – as their foot soldiers, pawns, cannon fodder. It wasn't pleasant. They had their own areas of responsibility and if you worked solely in any such area you were happy, because you had one boss. But if you, like me, had to cross over frequently from one director's area into the other's, then life was made intolerable.

The two directors countermanded each other's orders, played dirty tricks on each other, wouldn't speak to each other and generally behaved like very small children. I learnt, and learnt fast, to be a diplomat and a tactician. One director worked upstairs and one downstairs. I was sent up and down and learnt to stop on the landing half way and stay there until each had forgotten what particular bit of interdepartmental warfare was going on. I also learned to play them off against each other to get what I wanted – but that was very naughty.

I guess that was about as bad as it got, but I've also worked in companies where the rivalry between departments was extreme and interfered with productivity, kept staff on edge and contributed, I think, to very high staff turnover. You would have thought the directors would have stopped it but in my first example you can see that even directors are capable of being very silly and childish.

Don't you go the same way. Steer well clear of the lot of it, if you want my advice. Be open and honest and upfront in all your dealings and then you will get a good reputation and no one will be able to accuse you of being underhand.

> # EVEN DIRECTORS ARE CAPABLE OF BEING VERY SILLY AND CHILDISH

RULE 95

Show that you'll fight to the death for your team

Your team is your tool for getting the job done – whatever it happens to be. Without your team – and that can be one lone person or thousands of people – you are nothing. Without your team you are an empty page waiting to be written – or typed. You must support your team, praise it, fight for it – to the death if need be. The brilliant manager – we don't need to say who that is by now, do we? – generates loyalty and respect by being the team cheerleader – that's you, that is.

You have to make people in your team see that you are not only their mentor, leader, guardian and protector but also their champion, their hero, their defender. If anyone tries to criticize them you will rise to their defence. If anyone tries to take advantage of them you will rush to protect them.

> ## WITHOUT YOUR TEAM
> ## YOU ARE AN EMPTY PAGE
> ## WAITING TO BE WRITTEN

On the other hand you could always throw them to the wolves. See how far it gets you. But there are a lot of managers out there who seem to think that's the clever option, the right choice. What do you think? I've worked for and with some, and, believe me, they lose staff so fast.

If your staff have seen you defend them once, they will know they can trust you to have their best interests at heart. That if something unfair is being imposed on them, you will stand up for them. This also means that if you accept something, they are likely to accept it too – which makes for a smoother life all round.

Aim for respect rather than being liked

God, don't you just hate the manager who tries to be your chum, one of the lads/girls, your mate, your pal? We've all worked with them and they are a mess. They embarrass themselves as much as their team. Aim for aloof. Aim for respect rather than being liked. Look, you want your staff to give you all they've got, not hugs and drinks down the pub. You want them to think you're a god, not David Brent.

You have to create mystique, an air of power, authority, friendliness, without the desperate need to be liked. You have to remain detached.

Some day you may have to sack some of these people, and you don't need to make it tougher on yourself than you have to.

Some day you will have to promote some of these people, and you don't want to be seen to be having favourites.

They've got to be able to look up to you, respect you, have you as a role model. They can't do that if you've been seen rolling around on the floor of the pub drunk as a skunk on a Friday evening, now can they? You can't create mystique if you try to be too chummy with them. Maintain a distance and they won't see it as stand-offishness but will respect the space you give them.

> ## YOU HAVE TO CREATE
> ## MYSTIQUE, AN AIR OF POWER

Maintain a physical aloofness as well: no back slapping, hugging, kissing, hair ruffling (hey, I had a manager who used to do this to me; I hated it and him – I was very young but that shouldn't have made any difference), arm wrestling (you could lose and you'd lose all respect then, believe me), office football, or any form of rough and tumble. Maintain your dignity at all times – and your style, credibility, sanity and authority.

Do one or two things well and avoid the rest

The really good manager is a specialist. You can't do everything. You can't do everyone's job. You can't do more than a few things each day anyway. Best to pick your specialist subject, be really, really good at it and leave the rest to other people. In my company we have a very clear demarcation of who does what. I try to do as little as possible. I figure the better a manager, the less you do; it's all down to your powers of delegation.

So I stick to what I do best, which is basically talking to other managers. I don't do sales but I do open doors for sales staff to walk through. I don't do key accounts but I do set up contacts for our key people to follow through, and I do oversee the accounting staff. My 'one or two things' is setting up meetings for my team to do the business, and overseeing the overall style of the company – its branding, its corporate identity, its place in the market. I manage the company but I don't do products.

> BEST TO PICK YOUR
> SPECIALIST SUBJECT, BE
> REALLY, REALLY GOOD
> AT IT AND LEAVE THE
> REST TO OTHER PEOPLE

I know my limitations. I know what I am good at and what I am bad at. I'm lousy on detail, routine, order, regular everyday stuff. I am good on sudden, unorthodox, interesting, one-off, people-orientated projects. I don't see what I am good at as being better, nor do I see the things I am bad at as being inferior. Quite the opposite in fact. I envy the ordered, those who can pay attention to detail, those who like to see a project through from beginning to end, those with empty in-trays and tidy desks.

What are you good at? And bad? How would you best describe the one or two things you could do well?

Seek feedback on your performance

Now usually we don't go round seeking approval because we can follow our gut instincts and we know when we have done a good job. But feedback is always a good thing. You should seek feedback from your peers, your rivals, your team, your bosses and your customers. You are not seeking praise, approval or love, merely feedback. Remember you are all in the same team – from the janitor right up to the CEO – all kicking towards the same goal, all waving the same flag, or should be.

You should seek feedback to:

- identify your strengths and weaknesses

- compare the feedback with your own assessment of any situation – to make sure you are on track and realistic with your own appraisal

- learn from a situation where you went wrong – or got it right – for next time

- identify problem areas that need action and over which you have responsibility

- see how your team is performing – as additional information to your own assessment.

See, none of this involves praise or approval (or love). It is a realistic appraisal of a situation or project so you can learn and move on.

Now, how do you ask for feedback? Well, asking people in the team is easy. 'So, team, how did we do?' They'll tell you all right.

Next, your boss. 'So, Boss, how did I do?' Again easy.

Customers? Easy. 'Is there anything we could do to improve the service/product/delivery times/specifications/proposal?' They'll tell you all right as well.

Colleagues? Just ask. 'So, could you give me some feedback on how you saw the relocation go off?' Or, 'Could you tell me how you think we (you and your team) did with the exhibition?' Or, 'Any chance of some feedback on the cost-cutting exercise/new accounting procedure/staffing levels over the summer holidays/new theme park ride?' Don't preface it with, 'Can you tell me where I went wrong?' or, 'I know the relocation went off appallingly but I don't know where we screwed up'. Or, even worse, 'Help me out here, can you, I done wrong but no one will tell me what I did?' Don't give anyone your judgement of the situation in advance. Let them tell you the good and the bad. Just nod at it all and say 'Thank you' and move on.

> LET THEM TELL YOU THE
> GOOD AND THE BAD. JUST
> NOD AT IT ALL AND SAY
> 'THANK YOU' AND MOVE ON

Maintain good relationships and friendships

I have a friend who has a catchphrase – don't we all? – and his is, 'I don't see how that can possibly be good manners'. He uses it if anyone talks across him at meetings or steals his ideas. I love it because it says everything about poor working relationships. Good manners – what a simple concept but how big a subject.

It is easy to maintain good relationships and friendships at work if you maintain good manners. This doesn't have to mean opening doors for people or carrying their suitcases. Good manners is being polite, warm, human, compassionate, helpful, welcoming – all the things you'd be for your customers, or should be (I'm sure you are).

This becomes tricky when it comes to somebody you don't like, have clashed with in the past or who has been rude or unpleasant to you. But that's when it's most important to use this skill.

Even the rudest and most unpleasant person will find it very hard to keep being rude if you are pleasant, smiling and open with them (especially if you can bear to throw in a little flattery about their expertise on a subject – if it's justified, of course).

Try to see your colleagues as if they were equally as warm as yourself. If you always approach everyone with cheerful optimism you'll find that they simply have no choice but to respond in kind. Offer help when you can. Speak to everyone as if they were your equal – as indeed they are. Look for the positive points in people – find something to like or respect about them and focus on that. Take as much time with the most modest of employees as you would with the highest. Treat everyone the same – with respect and decency.

IF YOU ALWAYS APPROACH
EVERYONE WITH CHEERFUL
OPTIMISM YOU'LL FIND
THAT THEY SIMPLY HAVE
NO CHOICE BUT TO
RESPOND IN KIND

RULE 100

Build respect – both ways – between you and your customers

I was listening to a double-glazing salesperson on the radio the other day and the way he was talking about his customers made me think he and they were different species. He was condescending, patronizing, abusive, belittling and ridiculing. He seemed to think it was fair to con people – he said it was up to us to check the small print and if we didn't we were somehow stupid.

I have no respect for such people because of these attitudes – and the fact they phone me most evenings as I sit down to dinner with my children. I have a whole range of techniques to punish them for this, including pretending to be deaf and making them shout, saying they need to speak to my father, and leaving the phone off the hook until they get bored and hang up.

Don't cheat or lie to your customers. You need them. It's a two-way thing and it is an important relationship. Customers are never too much trouble. They provide my food and clothing and smart car and good holidays. Why should I abuse them? In return, I provide them with entertainment, fun, quality products, a brand they can be proud of, a lifestyle they can buy into, and a sense of belonging to an exciting and dynamic company. I respect them for what they give me and they respect me for what I give them.

DON'T CHEAT OR LIE TO
YOUR CUSTOMERS.
YOU NEED THEM

RULE 101

Go the extra mile for your customers

This is the easiest Rule of all. Going the extra mile should be the first thing on your mind when you wake in the morning and the last thing at night. Everything you do should be to take service that bit further.

Trouble is, customers are such a pain in the backside. They want stuff, they demand, they are difficult, they complain, they call at unnatural hours, they expect service above and beyond, they think the whole damn business should be run for them, they moan when we move our call centre to India, they want money off, free gifts, two for one, buy one get one free, money back if they are dissatisfied, replacement products, guarantees, safety checks, harmless products. God, who do they think they are? Strike a chord here? Ring any bells? I've worked in industries where the customer wasn't so much king as an inconvenience.

Let's clear up one thing here and now. Without the customer there is no point. No point coming in. No point making anything. No point creating anything. No point doing anything. Without the customer we are all whistling in the dark.

> ## WITHOUT THE CUSTOMER WE ARE ALL WHISTLING IN THE DARK

OK, point made. Now we realize the importance of customers, we have to think of ways of getting them, keeping them, satisfying them, welcoming them, going the extra mile for them. We don't have to be toadies but we do have to be creative in the ways we woo them. It's a lot cheaper to service an existing customer than to recruit a new one. Keep the ones you've got by being nice to them. Quick exercise: think of three ways of going the extra mile for your customer right now.

Be aware of your responsibilities

As a manager you have a responsibility to people in your team. You must make sure they don't come to harm while they are in your care. You have to make sure they are safe, healthy, cared for, well fed and watered, comfortable, kept well away from hazardous substances and equipment, and that they wear suitable safety clothing if necessary.

Now you also have a responsibility to the environment in much the same way. You mustn't do anything that is going to do harm, cause lasting damage, put anyone at risk of health or life, cause any land to be utilized in a worse way than it was before you came along. You don't have to be an eco-warrior but you do have a responsibility not to cause harm or damage. Can you put your hand on your heart and say your managerial role is 'clean'?

You have to have some principles – that you won't cause harm or damage. There has to be a line drawn – by you – somewhere, beyond which you will not go. You have to give something back. You have to be aware of what is going on around you. You have to be aware of what your industry contributes – or takes – from the environment.

This isn't stuff from the fairies or the hippies or the karmic religionists – this is real stuff. The more you put in, the more you get out. Be good and sleep nights. It's not a bad philosophy to live by and to manage with.

CAN YOU PUT YOUR HAND
ON YOUR HEART AND SAY
YOUR MANAGERIAL
ROLE IS 'CLEAN'?

Be straight at all times and speak the truth

This Rule follows right on from the previous Rule. Obviously if you think your boss is an idiot you don't go and tell them – that's taking honesty just a shade too far. But don't lie, or cheat, or steal, or abuse, or defraud, or take advantage, or con, or trick, or swindle, or hinder, or worsen.

As a manager you have been given a privileged position – one of trust and honour. You are responsible for human lives – no, really, real human lives. You screw up and people get hurt. When they go home after working for you all day they carry on living and breathing, feeling and loving, hurting and dreaming and hoping. You upset them or offend them or abuse them or lie to them and they take that home and it affects their close family and friends and relatives. You must speak the truth to them at all times. If you can't say anything nice, say nothing, but don't lie.

> ## AS A MANAGER YOU HAVE BEEN GIVEN A PRIVILEGED POSITION – ONE OF TRUST AND HONOUR

Don't lie to your bosses. They don't employ you to do that. They employ you to be straight and to tell the truth. If you're not going to make your figures, don't fudge the issue – tell them. They can then take measures to help you or take action because you not making your figures might have knock-on effects. They might be let down but they will be grateful for the warning. Better to know, than to hope and be disappointed.

Don't lie to customers. Obviously in all this there is a measure of artistic truth telling. If a customer asks if your products are superior to your competitors' you don't have to lie because they are – or you'd be working for the competition, wouldn't you? But if they ask if certain products have been successful and they haven't you are entitled to creative truth telling. Say, 'We have been somewhat surprised by sales so far but there is always room for improvement', rather than, 'These really bombed but we're hoping you'll take a load off our hands'.

RULE 104

Don't cut corners – you'll get found out

Maybe you make aeroplanes – are you going to cut corners? Maybe use substandard metal in the wings? Replace the engines with junkyard replacements? I don't think so. You'd get found out pretty quick. Hey, there is an increasing trend of taking managers to court if they have been responsible for injury to anyone using one of their products which has been found to be faulty (by way of design or manufacture or cost cutting). Quite right too. If we were all made to be personally responsible for what we do in our working lives maybe things would get a whole lot better. Rant over.

Maybe you don't make aeroplanes. Maybe you don't make anything. Maybe you just program computers. Nice and safe. Can't hurt anyone there, can you? No? Sure? Think things through. Work out worst-case scenarios and be prepared for the fact that whatever we do as managers, we are responsible for someone or something that could get damaged, hurt, wounded, upset, impaired, killed – you name it.

Cutting corners ain't worth it – you'll always get found out. Sod's law. I know you can get caught between the devil and the deep blue sea at times, with your boss telling you to do something and your principles telling you it is madness, but you need the job and the mortgage has to be paid and it's easier to shut up and pretend it's all all right. But it ain't. You'll get found out.

And you have to move heaven and earth to prove to your boss that cutting corners is a real waste of time. The old, 'But what would the media/auditors make of this if they got hold of it?' argument often works wonders. As does asking about what insurance we carry or how the legal department has viewed this cost-cutting exercise. If you get told, 'I haven't bothered running it past them', you can clap your hand to your head and shriek, 'Oh, no, I'm working with a mad person'. Using humour can get someone else to realize they have overstepped the mark and need to think.

> **IF WE WERE ALL MADE TO BE PERSONALLY RESPONSIBLE FOR WHAT WE DO IN OUR WORKING LIVES MAYBE THINGS WOULD GET A WHOLE LOT BETTER**

RULE 105

Find the right sounding board

Management isn't easy. I mean, sometimes it all goes swimmingly, but sooner or later you come up against a tricky problem – handling someone difficult, finding the best way to address a particular challenge, deciding how to spread the budget around most effectively.

What you need is another pair of ears – a sounding board. It needs to be someone who understands the issues, so probably someone in the company. On the other hand you shouldn't really be talking about these things with junior colleagues, especially if they involve other managers. But sometimes you don't really want to discuss it with your boss – definitely not a good idea if your boss is the subject matter.

It can be tricky to find the right person, but it's important that you consciously seek out someone you can talk to. Otherwise you will find some challenges much harder than necessary, and you'll also risk becoming so frustrated that you talk to the wrong people.

Your best bet is generally a manager as senior as you but in a different department. You need someone discreet who you can trust, and whose judgement you respect, and who will find time for you – it's no good if they're never there. And of course it's ideal if it can be reciprocal. You can both support each other, and that makes the trust thing much more balanced. No one's going to blab to your boss about what you said if they've also confided in you.

You don't have to limit yourself to one sounding board of course. It's not going to work if you discuss the more confidential aspects of your job with dozens of people. Even if they can all be discreet, which is unlikely – almost everyone will know your innermost worries and weaknesses and you don't want that. However, you may find that you have a couple of peers who are useful sounding boards – maybe one who is very helpful over staff issues and another who has a really clear head for strategy. And sometimes someone outside the organization can give you a better perspective because they aren't bogged down in too much detail, in the way you are. Maybe your partner or a close friend or your mum or an ex-colleague. Someone who will give you a new angle on things.

> YOU NEED SOMEONE
> DISCREET WHO YOU
> CAN TRUST, AND WHOSE
> JUDGEMENT YOU RESPECT,
> AND WHO WILL FIND
> TIME FOR YOU

Be in command and take charge

You are a manager, so manage. Managing means just that, managing. Managing to work effectively. Managing to be in charge. Managing to be in command.

There seems to be a new movement in which managers are frightened to take command. They seem reluctant to assume control in case their team might resent this or accuse them of being a dictator. Nothing could be further from the truth. Teams with good, strong, commanding managers go a lot further because they know there is a captain at the helm. Without a captain we are all at sea – lost, scared, about to crash on the rocks. In a way it almost doesn't matter what captain we've got, just so long as we've got someone with their hand on the rudder. We all know the first mate does all the real sailing anyway, so the captain can be whatever, but the first mate can't function unless they know there is someone there, at the helm.

You've got to be a hero to your team and a good second-in-command to your boss. You have to be all these old-fashioned things:

- dependable
- reliable
- strong
- trustworthy
- faithful
- loyal
- staunch
- dedicated
- accountable.

Boy, it's all a tall order, a tough call. But the rewards are immense. Being a manager is a fabulous job if you handle it right, abide by the rules and play it straight.

> TEAMS WITH GOOD, STRONG, COMMANDING MANAGERS GO A LOT FURTHER BECAUSE THEY KNOW THERE IS A CAPTAIN AT THE HELM

Be a diplomat for the company

I hope you don't have to 'kiss butts' to be a diplomat for your company, but diplomat you should be. The company you work for will drive you mad at times, and at others please you no end. If you can stay away from the politics and backbiting that goes on in any organization, you'll be doing fine. Accept that every company has bad bits and good bits. Focus on the good bits and be incredibly proud that they had the good sense to employ one of the best managers in the business – you.

Speak highly of your company wherever you go and in whatever you do. This will get back to head office and make you even more proud, because nothing generates pride better than being proud (the opposite of a vicious circle – a kindly circle?).

If you get a complaint, accept it, tell the person you will investigate and get back to them – and do it.

Having to be a diplomat makes you question what your company represents – and that makes you question how happy you are working for them. If it is good and you are already proud – good for you. But if you have doubts you might have to do some soul searching before continuing. Don't chuck in the towel immediately – you might be of more use on the inside, changing from there.

Just as you would go that extra mile for a customer, find ways to go that extra mile for your company. This doesn't mean you have to be a yes-person or a lackey or a doormat. You can be strong, proud, independent, rebellious and still be a diplomat for the company.

HAVING TO BE A DIPLOMAT MAKES YOU QUESTION WHAT YOUR COMPANY REPRESENTS

THE RULES FOR ENTREPRENEURS

If you're thinking or planning or, at this stage, just dreaming of starting your own business, I hope you've digested the Rules of management, but hold on to your hat – you're not done yet. There are some additional Rules that apply specifically to entrepreneurs.

When you run your own business, you have to think very differently from the way you think when you work for someone else. Obviously you have to understand different things – you may never have needed to consider finance before, or production, or sales. But it's more than that. You have to see the business from a very different perspective.

It's thrillingly exciting starting your own business, or it should be – that's my experience anyway – and it's easy to get caught up in your passion for the new product or service or market that you're developing. Quite right too. But you need to keep a very clear management head at the same time, and learn (fast) to stop thinking like a manager and start thinking like an entrepreneur.

There's a huge amount to learn when you set up a new company for the first time. That's a lot of the fun of doing it. And there's a lot of practical advice available. However, I've known, watched and worked with a lot of entrepreneurs over the years, and it's clear to me that there's a set of principles that separate the happy successful business owners from those who find it all a massive struggle. That's what you'll find here. The real gold dust; the often unspoken Rules that successful entrepreneurs follow and unsuccessful ones don't.

RULE 1

Don't borrow money

You'll argue with this Rule, and you'll be quite right. It's more of an aspiration than an outright Rule. I realize that sometimes you have a great business idea that needs more funds than you can provide yourself. However, I want to persuade you that you should only go down this route if there's no alternative.

I have a friend who started a business with a mate. They had a great idea, approached venture capitalists successfully, and launched their company. It did brilliantly and six years later they sold it for £6 million. Of course, the venture capitalists owned most of the company and my friend came away with a couple of hundred thousand. Very nice, but nowhere near what his backers made.

Another friend started a company with three other people. They each put up a quarter of the money. They started small and reinvested their profits in the business. Like my other friend, they built a successful and acclaimed company. Twenty years later, they sold the business for £40 million. How much did they come away with? Yep, £40 million. Sure they had to pay tax on it, and there were some legal and accounting costs in selling the company, but they ended up pocketing the money they'd worked so hard to make.

Even if you take out a loan rather than selling equity, you're then left servicing that loan, which will eat up your profits – profits you wanted to put back into the business. Nevertheless, a loan beats venture capital almost every time.

Now I accept that some business ideas really do need a lot of backing and there's no alternative – except not starting the business in the first place. Even if you make less money out of it in the end, you'll have enjoyed the process and the freedom of being in control, and you'll still have something to show for it when you sell, even if it's a small proportion of the sale price. So I'm not saying you should never start a business if you can't fund it yourself. But recognize that it's not the no-brainer many of the books and advisors out there will imply.

Explore all the alternatives before you look for outside money. And if you decide to borrow from family, think very carefully through the potential repercussions if things go wrong. For the same reason, never sink your house, life savings, inheritance or anything similar into a new venture without the full support of your partner.

The interesting thing about those two examples I just gave you is that the two companies were in broadly the same line of business. The first one wanted to make a splash by launching onto the market with a wide range of products. Actually, the second one *wanted* to do the same thing, but because of their decision to fund themselves, they started up with just one solitary product. But it sold. So they used the profits to add another two products to their range, and so on. And look at the difference that approach made. They could retire when they sold their business, while the first pair of entrepreneurs had to carry on working.

So before you start looking for other people's money to fund your enterprise, be absolutely certain that there's no alternative. It's pretty galling to sell up after years of hard graft and hand the hard-earned money over to someone else.

> THEY ENDED UP POCKETING
> THE MONEY THEY'D WORKED
> SO HARD TO MAKE

RULE 2

Find a balance

Starting your own business is pretty all-consuming. It takes up most of your time, and when you're not doing it, you're thinking about it. Of course it should be enormous fun – despite the intermittent worries – so you probably won't begrudge the time you give to it.

Oh, yes, there are worries. They go with the territory up to a point. But aside from the question of whether you'll clinch this deal, or how the new product line will go down, there is another underlying cause for anxiety. There is a level of insecurity which goes with being an entrepreneur that is like nothing you've experienced as an employee. No one is paying you, there's no pension fund unless you create it, and there's no absolute guarantee that the work won't dry up tomorrow. If it all falls apart, you'll not only be out of a job, you may also be left with sizeable debts.

I'm not trying to depress you. Some people thrive on this kind of life – they feel free and unfettered and enjoy controlling their own destiny – while others just can't shake the feeling of insecurity, and they worry all the time, sometimes to the point where they simply don't enjoy themselves even when things are going well. I've seen both scenarios many times, and before you launch your own business you need to be sure that you'll be happy living without the trappings of a secure job. Otherwise your whole life suffers, and you may struggle to cope both in and out of work.

OK, so you're feeling free to do your own thing, and happy to risk the ups and downs of running a business. Obviously the more hours you put into the business, the more confident you can be that all will be well. And there are always piles of things to get on with, because as an entrepreneur it's your job to be proactive, to initiate projects, dream up new products or services, chase fresh deals. Yep, always lots to do.

If you're young and single this is great. You can plough your soul into the operation if you want to. But what if you have a family, kids, ageing parents – they need some of your time too. It's scary how easily marriages fall apart when one partner runs their own business. Or how often friends have told me they wish they'd spent more time with the kids or with their parents when they had their own business.

I've run a business with my partner. It doesn't work for everyone but it does help to prevent the business breaking up the marriage. However, it doesn't get you any more time with the children. You need firm boundaries.* Our rule, when the kids were small, was no working after 6pm or at weekends *no matter what*. Which we (mostly) stuck to. You can pick your own system, but if you start to bend the rules, you're on a downward slope. You have to be disciplined about this if you want your partnership to last and your relationship with your children to thrive. But if you can make it work, you'll have the most fun and rewarding life you could hope for.

> # THERE IS A LEVEL OF INSECURITY WHICH GOES WITH BEING AN ENTREPRENEUR THAT IS LIKE NOTHING YOU'VE EXPERIENCED AS AN EMPLOYEE

---

* Yes, you, never mind the kids . . .

Plan for the worst

Sorry if this is depressing, but somehow things never go according to plan. Unless, of course, you've planned for the worst. If you know how to weather tough conditions, you'll cope far better when they happen along. Which they will.

I've seen so many businesses fold because the owners had no Plan B for if it took longer than they thought to become profitable (which it always does, by the way), or if a major customer went bust, or if the economy hit recession. I knew one man who spent years building up a really strong business, most of whose clients were in the banking and building industries – both of which tanked at the same time and took him out too. It was heartbreaking to see.

Lots of businesses go under during a recession – and losing your business is usually even worse than losing your job – but those that survive come out the other side lean and mean and become successful. And they do it by being prepared for the worst. Make sure this is your business, even when you can't see any clouds on the horizon. A storm can brew fast out of a clear blue sky.

For a start, always assume it will take you at least three years to become profitable, no matter what your business plan and your cash flow forecast tell you. No, I don't know why it necessarily should but somehow it just does, even if you can't see how. Of course you read stories in the press about people whose idea just hits the zeitgeist and orders pour in faster than they can cope, but this is incredibly rare – that's why it makes the news. It's often presented by the media as coming from nowhere, but in reality it's always backed by a lot of clever thinking, hard work, canny marketing and a good dose of plain luck. Never assume this will happen to you. Certainly not the luck bit.

So how to plan for the unknown? You need to analyze your businesses strengths and, especially, weaknesses. Are you very reliant on one or two big clients? What would happen if raw materials prices rocketed? Suppose next season's line just isn't as popular as past ones? What if someone else starts up in competition with you? What if key personnel (for example, you) become ill and have to take weeks or months off work? What if the economy goes into freefall? What if new technology is developed that supersedes yours? What if you have a computer disaster?

Not all these things are going to happen simultaneously, but sooner or later at least one or two of them will, and as you've no idea which one or two it will be, you need to have sat down and planned a strategy to cope with each of your business's potential threats. Once you've done that, you should be able to sleep better.

ALWAYS ASSUME IT WILL TAKE YOU AT LEAST THREE YEARS TO BECOME PROFITABLE

RULE 4

Have a mission

What are mission statements all about then? Just self-indulgent bits of marketing twaddle? Or do they actually serve some purpose? Until I first ran my own business, I'd looked at mission statements from other companies and been deeply cynical about them. And indeed some of them are badly thought through and churned out for PR purposes in a way that deserves all the scepticism any of us can muster.

However, don't let a few bad, or badly used, examples put you off the concept of a mission statement. It's actually essential to your business, I promise. The more succinct and straightforward it is, the better. So what is it for? Well, it's a statement of the absolute core, central purpose of your business. The reason it exists. The justification for its place in the world. Let me give you an example of a couple of the best – and rightly best-known – mission statements, to show you what I mean:

- Disney – To make people happy.

- Wal-Mart – To give ordinary folk the chance to buy the same things as rich people.

- 3M – To solve unsolved problems innovatively.

One of the most important bits of your mission statement is the mental process of writing it. As you can see from those examples, you have to really focus on exactly what it is your company is all about. It's a harder process than you might think, and an absolutely essential one.

Once you have honed the statement to encapsulate perfectly what your business is for, you can use it in your planning. Should we branch into this or that product line? Check it against your mission statement to see if it's relevant to the core business. Is this is a useful direction to invest our profits? Does it meet the criteria set out in the mission statement? And so on. It's your touchstone to check against when you're planning to see that you stay focused and on track.

The business plan is much the same, although it's more fluid. Of course it holds much more detail than a mission statement, and it can be modified when necessary to reflect changes in the business or simply to keep it rolling. If you don't borrow money, you can of course start an enterprise without a business plan at all, but I don't recommend it. Again, it makes you think about the things you should be thinking about but otherwise probably wouldn't.

Loads of start-ups put together a business plan and then never look at it again once they've got their funding. Which is plain daft, as they're missing out on a wealth of useful planning information. However, since a business plan changes over time, if you don't update it you won't have that valuable resource at your fingertips for long. And you'll be less likely to keep your eye on the big picture as time goes on. I'll leave you with a statistic that I hope will make the point clearly: over 90 per cent of businesses that fail had no written business plan. Enough said.

> YOU HAVE TO REALLY FOCUS
> ON EXACTLY WHAT IT IS YOUR
> COMPANY IS ALL ABOUT

RULE 5

Be brutally honest

Look, no one can be brilliant at everything. How many people do you know who are great at seeing the big picture and yet also have a real eye for detail? Which ideas powerhouses do you know who are also good at dealing with day-to-day admin? They simply don't go together. It just isn't possible to be an all-round genius, and if you fall into the trap of thinking that you are, your business is doomed.

Some entrepreneurs think the things they aren't personally good at aren't so important. Maybe they realize that's not true if, say, they don't like doing figures. But if their own skills don't really include strong customer relations, or quality control, or negotiating, or selecting staff, or software skills, or budgeting, they underrate the importance of those aspects of the business.

Maybe your weak points are along those lines, or perhaps (*and perhaps?*) they are in crossover skills such as dealing with people, or making decisions, or seeing things through, or training people well, or delegating. If you don't address these, you can add another weakness to your list: not knowing your own limitations. And, trust me, that's something that can break a small business.

You have to understand that it is normal to have shortcomings, especially when it comes to business. This is not a reflection on your value as a human being, simply on the set of skills at your disposal. When you work in a big corporation, it probably doesn't matter because you can play to your strengths and other people can compensate for your weaknesses, just as you can compensate for theirs.

Running your own business doesn't work like that. It's your job to have every role covered. No, of course you don't have to magically acquire the ability to cover them all yourself. You can find ways around your own weaknesses. Except you can't do that if you haven't faced up to what they are.

I've said you have to be brutal, so I'll start you off . . . Think about this. There's no shame in using an outside payroll provider, or a part-time finance manager or branding consultant. There's no shame in appointing a customer care manager or a PA. There's no shame in reading up on negotiating skills or signing up to a course on how to take effective decisions. But you *should* be ashamed of yourself if your business fails because you were too pig-headed to acknowledge your own shortcomings.

> # IT JUST ISN'T POSSIBLE TO BE AN ALL-ROUND GENIUS

RULE 6

Get all the help you can

Right. Now you've been brutally honest you'll know what you can't do yourself. Plus, since you only have a finite number of hours each day, you may not be able to do even the stuff you are good at on your own. As time goes on, you'll find you need additional skills that you either don't have or don't have time to use – you need to plan an exhibition stand, or write material for clients, or the finances become more complex, or you start exporting.

So here's a problem. There's work for a dozen people but only you actually there – or perhaps two or three of you. And no money to pay anyone else. So what are you going to do? Actually, this is a good thing. Yes, I promise. We've already established that no one can do everything, and I don't have to know anything about you or your business to be able to tell you that you'll achieve far more with other people around you than you will on your own. You just have to be canny about getting help without paying out money you don't have.

There are some fairly obvious solutions, which can often work, such as taking people on part time, or on a one-off project basis, rather than creating an unaffordable full-time post. One option of course is to bring someone in as a partner in the business. Give them a share in the company and they'll work as hard as you do, and have a vested interest in paying themselves only what the company can afford. This is a great idea if you can find the right person with skills you'll always need – for example, if you've developed a great product but just don't get the whole marketing and sales thing. That's always going to be essential to the company's survival, and it's better to own 50 per cent of a successful company than 100 per cent of one that fails. But be wary of giving away equity if it isn't essential. Pick them carefully too because you'll be stuck with them.

Then there are costs you can share with other companies. For example, if you find another business with complementary but not competing products, you could exhibit at half the trade shows each and promote both sets of products on one stand. That saves time as well as splitting the costs of attending. There are lots of things you can share with the right fellow businesses in fact, from mailshots to information, bulk materials costs to sales leads.

And there's one more really important source of help I want to draw your attention to, because it's behind many successful new enterprises. Sometimes you think you need someone to do a job, when all you actually need is their expertise. Then you can do the job yourself. So put together an advisory panel of people who between them have experience in marketing, finance, production, PR, your particular product or service, and so on. Some people can tick more than one box – that helps but it's not essential.

The panel can be formal or informal, it can meet regularly or just be on the end of a phone. Pick the right people (friends, ex-colleagues, business contacts, whoever fits the bill – but keep the panel to a manageable size) and you shouldn't need to pay them, at least not to start with. Make them feel valued and important, don't ask too much time of each one, buy them the occasional slap-up thank you meal, and most people will enjoy it enough not to want paying. Then pick their brains every time you need their experience or intuition.

> ## SOMETIMES YOU THINK YOU NEED SOMEONE TO DO A JOB, WHEN ALL YOU ACTUALLY NEED IS THEIR EXPERTISE

RULE 7

Set up a strong culture

You're not working for a big corporation now. Or a small one. You're not working for anyone. You are the boss, the top banana, the head honcho, the big cheese, commander-in-chief. You call the shots.

Sooner or later, when your business grows, you'll actually have people working for you. You'll be employing staff of your own. Maybe one part-timer to begin with, then later on a few full-timers, and eventually you might have layers of management under you. All very gratifying, even if you're not an egomaniac.

It's going to be a gradual process. You won't necessarily notice it happening – you'll just wake up one day and realize that while you've been thinking about other things, you've become a people manager. You may not even particularly enjoy it, but you can't do much about it if you want your business to grow.

So. What sort of boss are you going to be? Are you going to crack the whip and sack anyone who turns up to work two minutes late? Are you going to be kind and caring and let staff take off all the time they need to cope with personal crises? Will you walk the floor regularly? Will you opt for a flat management model with no hierarchy?

You need to think about this now – whatever stage you're at. You'll probably start with one or two staff, and you may be inclined to treat them more as mates, so long as you know you can trust them not to take advantage. That will become a habit and then, when you wake up on that morning and realize you've got 20 people working for you – or 50, or 200 – you might wish you hadn't allowed that kind of culture to develop. Or you might be happy with it. I don't know – but you need to know. You need to have thought about it from the off and set up the management style you want.

Being the top boss is not the same as being a manager in someone else's company. You are responsible (legally as well as morally and practically) for the decisions you make. And you create the corporate culture. Listen, you've worked in companies where everyone helped everyone else, or where management were unapproachable, or where people were very considerate, or where there was lots of competition or backbiting, or where staff felt really well cared for, or where everyone was terrified of 'the boss', or where people milked the system.

This time it's down to you. Company culture comes down from the top. The pattern you set with those first one or two part-timers is going to grow with the business. Don't leave it to chance – make sure you create the company you want. And hey, you're a Rules player. I know you'll want a culture that's caring but professional, where everyone does their best and mistakes are accepted so long as they're learnt from, and the boss is passionate, approachable and respected by everyone. Yes, that's you.

> # SO. WHAT SORT OF BOSS ARE YOU GOING TO BE?

RULE 8

Don't say yes to everything

A friend of mine had a small publishing business. She was thrilled to be offered a deal for one of her books by one of the very biggest supermarket chains in the UK. They wanted to order tens of thousands of books from her. It was the kind of deal that even big publishers would drool over. After the initial euphoria wore off, she sat down and did some figures.

And in the end, she turned the deal down. A lot of her friends in bigger publishers thought she was mad, but she was just being level-headed. You see, the unit price the supermarket was offering was low, obviously. Not only that, but the book industry works on a sale or return basis. So any books they didn't sell would be returned and not paid for. Since they were ordering thousands of books, they could end up returning thousands – which could eat up all her profit from the deal, and more besides. A big publisher might be able to risk such a loss, but she couldn't.

If you've worked for a big organization before starting up on your own, don't fall into the trap of seeing things from a big company viewpoint. You need to analyze every deal from your own perspective, and some of them won't look nearly as promising as they first appeared.

I'll give you another example. Every industry and country has its own laws and systems and legislation and procedures and registration requirements. And all of these entail paperwork (ugh). Once you run your own business, you suddenly realize fully the meaning of the saying 'time is money'. You don't have to do your paperwork yourself, of course, but if you don't you'll have to pay someone else to do it. And the longer it takes, the more that'll cost you.

There are generally additional procedures – for which read additional paperwork – that kick in once you meet a certain number of employees, or level of turnover, or quantity of waste materials. Some suppliers or customers will insist on documentation you didn't need before; some foreign exports require complex admin procedures that other countries don't; some raw materials demand special protocols.

It's easy to get sucked into these things without realizing the implications in terms of admin, and then find yourself bogged down in paperwork and having to hire people to cope with it – or stay up half the night trying to work through it yourself.

Of course it's worth it sometimes, but sometimes it's not. So you need to think about the increase in admin that goes along with every change – adding staff, saying yes to a big customer, using new materials, exporting elsewhere, buying your own delivery vehicle, and all the rest.

All that glitters is not gold. Some new contracts turn out to be millstones. So get excited about new prospects – that's half the thrill of having your own business – but don't say yes until you've thought through *all* the implications. Even the boring admin-y ones. It's generally much harder to backtrack from these deals than it is to avoid them in the first place.

> # YOU NEED TO ANALYZE EVERY DEAL FROM YOUR OWN PERSPECTIVE

RULE 9

Stick by your decisions

Lots of entrepreneurs are creative types. Nothing wrong with that. Except that sometimes creative people can be unorganized. The positive way of looking at this is that they're dynamic, organic, mercurial. Or to put it another way – all over the shop.

Yep, butterfly minds, flitting hither and thither: 'Shall I try this flower or that flower? Ooh, that looks pretty, oh, hang on, maybe the last one was better.' To give a business example, 'I think I'll have a colour booklet, oh, actually maybe I'll just put it online – no, perhaps I *will* print it. But just 12 pages then. Or actually maybe a poster would be better . . . '

Now if you can go through this thought process in your head in a few minutes, and then settle on your 'flower', that's fine. But that's not generally what happens. I'll tell you a secret – most web designers hate working with start-ups. Why? Because they keep changing their minds. You give them exactly what they asked for, and they have second thoughts and change the brief. And then third thoughts, and on and on.

I'm not telling you this because I have a soft spot for web designers and I want to make their lives easier. No, it's you I'm trying to help. Listen, if you keep changing your mind, you'll spend money you probably can't spare, and certainly could have spent more wisely. Those web designers may be driven to distraction by your inconsistency, but in the end they'll be OK because they'll just charge you for all the extra time you've cost them. It's you who'll be out of pocket.

You'll miss deadlines too if you can't settle on a plan. That website, for a start, will take far longer to get up and running. Along with everything else from choosing premises to organizing your big launch event or getting products through development. And people will start to hate working with you because they can't get on with their jobs when you keep moving their goalposts. I've known plenty of entrepreneurs whose staff really liked them as people, but still kept leaving their employment in droves because they couldn't take the frustration and stress. Mercurial managers forget to tell people things they need to know, or forget to mention that they've changed the brief. So everything takes longer, and suppliers put up their prices, and customers get bored waiting for new products to come online.

So be creative – I know, you can't help it anyway. There's *always* going to be a better idea round the corner, or at least a fresher one, but you have to close the door on them at some point, fix your decision in concrete, and start putting it into action. From that point on, you trust your own decision, stick with what you've got and simply fine-tune it.

> # IF YOU KEEP CHANGING YOUR MIND, YOU'LL SPEND MONEY YOU CAN'T SPARE

RULE 10

Your time is everyone's time

I used to work for a guy who had a small company, very successful, very dynamic. The kind of company that gained an advantage from being able to make decisions faster than the big lumbering competitors in the market. Consequently his business grew rapidly, and by the time I started working for him, there were about 40 of us in the company. I stayed around a year, by which time there were 60. And the business was grinding along so slowly it had lost its advantage entirely. So what happened?

The owner had made a very easy but critical mistake – he hadn't changed his management style as his organization grew. He was still managing it just as he had when it started. Listen, when you have half a dozen employees you can look over all their shoulders and sign off on all their decisions. Hey, it's your business, your money, you need to be sure they're getting it right.

Trouble is, if you keep doing that as the business grows, you get spread thinner and thinner. A big organization has more activity, more decisions, more products, more meetings. You can't get involved in every one because there isn't time. And how you manage your own time affects how the whole company manages its time.

The reason I only stayed in that company for a year was because I couldn't stand the frustration. And I was far from being the only one who left. The owner started haemorrhaging staff. You see, we fought to get him to sign off on any decisions because he was so busy micro-managing everyone else, or he changed his mind after finally making decisions (see previous Rule). All of which meant we couldn't get on with our jobs, we missed deadlines, we let down customers and suppliers, cheques took ages to issue (signing cheques never seemed as urgent to him as all the other stuff on his to-do list) and everything started to stagnate. He was a lovely guy and we all liked him – he recognized he was slowing things up and never blamed us for the delays, but somehow he never did anything about it either.

So what should you do when your company grows? What should my old boss have done? Well, you need to have people around you that you trust – that's essential – and then delegate to them. It's much, much harder than you think to hand over decisions about your own company than it was when you worked for someone else. But if you want your business to thrive, you have to do it. Just put your hands in the air and step away from the detail. Concentrate on the big picture, the critical decisions, the direction of travel. Only manage the crucial people at the top of your company, and let *them* manage everyone else.

Once you've mastered that skill, you'll free up your staff to get on with their jobs, yourself to concentrate on the decisions that really matter, and your enterprise to grow and flourish.

> # HOW YOU MANAGE YOUR OWN TIME AFFECTS HOW THE WHOLE COMPANY MANAGES ITS TIME

End game

OK, no more Rules. This is your book. Keep it secret, keep it safe. If you don't let anyone else look at it you'll be one step ahead without having to do anything else.

I have enjoyed being a manager immensely, both in other people's organizations and as an entrepreneur. It has brought me great satisfaction as well as considerable stress at times. But it has always been an adventure, always exciting.

Over the years I have discovered these fundamental Rules, which I don't think you'll ever get taught at a manager's training weekend or course. These Rules have sustained and kept me through many years, from a humble junior manager right up to CEO of my own company. I hope they will serve you as well.

I don't expect you to learn them all, do them all, agree with them all. But they serve as a useful stepping-off point for conscious decision making, conscious management. What they won't do is turn you into a goody-goody.

When I was researching this book I talked to many other managers and entrepreneurs to see what secret Rules they lived by and was astounded to find a great many still lived by the 'stitch 'em up, stab 'em in the back, claw your way to the top' school of thought. Sad really. They were all skinny and looked stressed, haunted and unable to relax. The others, by contrast, who live by these Rules, seemed happier, more relaxed and much more at ease with themselves and with their staff – and their staff respected them and enjoyed working for them and with them. Much better.

Good luck with it all.

IT HAS ALWAYS BEEN
AN ADVENTURE,
ALWAYS EXCITING

HAD
ENOUGH
YET...?

Hey, it's not only management, you know. If you're smart, you'll want to learn how the most successful people behave at whatever it is: life, money, work, relationships, kids. Luckily I've done the hard work for you – the years of observing, the distilling and sieving and summarizing what really makes a difference into handy little Rules.

I've always been anxious not to stretch the Rules principle too far, but following huge demand from readers, I have tackled those big important areas that affect us all. So in the pages to follow you'll find a 'one Rule' taster of each of the other Rules books:

Rules of Life
Rules of Work
Rules of Wealth
Rules of Parenting
Rules of Love

See what you think. And if you like them there are plenty more in each of the books.

You'll get older but not necessarily wiser

There is an assumption that as we get older we will get wiser; not true, I'm afraid. The rule is we carry on being just as daft, still making plenty of mistakes. It's just that we make new ones, different ones. We do learn from experience and may not make the same mistakes again, but there is a whole new pickle jar of fresh ones just lying in wait for us to trip up and fall into. The secret is to accept this and not to beat yourself up when you do make new ones. The Rule really is: be kind to yourself when you do muck things up. Be forgiving and accept that it's all part of that growing older but no wiser routine.

Looking back, we can always see the mistakes we made, but we fail to see the ones looming up. Wisdom isn't about not making mistakes, but about learning to escape afterwards with our dignity and sanity intact.

When we are young, ageing seems to be something that happens to, well, old people. But it does happen to us all and we have no choice but to embrace it and roll with it. Whatever we do and however we are, the fact is we are going to get older. And this ageing process does seem to speed up as we get older.

You can look at it this way – the older you get, the more areas you've covered to make mistakes in. There will always be new areas of experience where we have no guidelines and where we'll handle things badly, overreact, get it wrong. And the more flexible we are, the more adventurous, the more life-embracing, then the more new avenues there will be to explore – and make mistakes in of course.

As long as we look back and see where we went wrong and resolve not to repeat such mistakes, there is little else we need to do. Remember that any Rules that apply to you also apply to everyone else around you. They are all getting older too. And not any wiser particularly. Once you accept this, you'll be more forgiving and kinder towards yourself and others.

Finally, yes, time does heal and things do get better as you get older. After all, the more mistakes you've made, the less likely that you'll come up with new ones. The best thing is that if you get a lot of your mistakes over and done with early on in life, there will be less to learn the hard way later on. And that's what youth is all about, a chance to make all the mistakes you can and get them out of the way.

> **WISDOM ISN'T ABOUT NOT MAKING MISTAKES BUT ABOUT LEARNING TO ESCAPE AFTERWARDS WITH OUR DIGNITY AND SANITY INTACT**

Get your work noticed

It's all too easy for your work to get overlooked in the busy hurly burly of office life. You're slaving away and it can be hard to remember that you need to put in some effort to boost your individual status and personal kudos for your work. But it's important. You have to make your mark so you stand out and your promotional potential will be realised.

The best way to do this is to step outside the normal working routine. If you have to process so many widgets each day – and so does everyone else – then processing more won't do you that much good. But if you submit a report to your boss of how everyone could process more widgets then you'll get noticed. The unsolicited report is a brilliant way to stand out from the crowd. It shows you're thinking on your feet and using your initiative. But it mustn't be used too often. If you subject your boss to a barrage of unsolicited reports, you'll get noticed but in completely the wrong way. You have to stick to certain rules:

- Only submit a report occasionally.

- Make really sure that your report will actually work – that it will do good or provide benefits.

- Make sure your name is prominently displayed.

- Make sure the report will be seen not only by your boss, but by their boss as well.

- Remember it doesn't have to be a report – it can be an article in the company newsletter.

Of course, the very best way to get your work noticed is to be very, very good at your job. And the best way to be good at your job is to be totally dedicated to doing the job and ignoring all the rest. There is a vast amount of politics, gossip, gamesmanship, time wasting and socializing that goes on in the name of work. It isn't work. Keep your eye on the ball and you'll already be playing with a vast advantage over your colleagues. The Rules Player stays focused. Keep your mind on the task at hand – being very good at your job – and don't get distracted.

> # THE UNSOLICITED REPORT IS
> # A BRILLIANT WAY TO STAND
> # OUT FROM THE CROWD

Anybody can be wealthy – you just need to apply yourself

The lovely thing about money is that it really doesn't discriminate. It doesn't care what colour or race you are, what class you are, what your parents did, or even who you *think* you are. Each and every day starts with a clean slate so that no matter what you did yesterday, today begins anew and you have the same rights and opportunities as everyone else to take as much as you want. The only thing that can hold you back is yourself and your own money myths.

> ## YOU HAVE THE SAME RIGHTS AND OPPORTUNITIES AS EVERYONE ELSE TO TAKE AS MUCH AS YOU WANT

Of the wealth of the world each has as much as they take. What else could make sense? There is no way money can know who is handling it, what their qualifications are, what ambitions they have or what class they belong to. Money has no ears or eyes or senses. It is inert, inanimate, impassive. It hasn't a clue. It is there to be used and spent, saved and invested, fought over, seduced with and worked for. It has no discriminatory apparatus so it can't judge whether you are 'worthy' or not.

I have watched a lot of extremely wealthy people and the one thing they all have in common is that they have nothing in common – apart from all being Rules Players of course. The wealthy are a diverse band of people – the least likely can be loaded. They vary from the genteel to the uncouth, the savvy to the plain stupid, the deserving to the undeserving. But each and every one of them has stepped up and said, 'Yes please, I want some of that.' And the poor are the ones saying, 'No thank you, not for me, I am not worthy. I am not deserving enough. I couldn't. I mustn't. I shouldn't.'

That's what this book is about, challenging your perceptions of money and the wealthy. We all assume the poor are poor because of circumstances, their background, their upbringing, their nurture. But if you have the means to buy a book such as this and live in comparative security and comfort in the world then you too have the power to be wealthy. It may be hard. It may be tough but it is doable. And that is Rule 1 – anyone can be wealthy, you just have to apply yourself. All the other Rules are about that application.

Relax

So who are the best parents you know? The ones who have a seemingly instinctive ability to say and do the things that will result in happy, confident, well-balanced children? Have you ever wondered what makes them so good at it? Now think about the ones you privately don't think are much cop. Why not?

All the best parents I know have one key thing in common. They're relaxed about it. And all the worst ones are hung up on something. Maybe they're not stressed out about how good they are as parents (perhaps they should be) but they're hung up about something that affects their ability to be a really good parent.

I know a couple of parents who are neurotically clean and tidy. Their children have to take their shoes off at the door or the whole world falls apart. Even if the shoes are clean. They get really uptight if their children leave anything out of place or make any kind of a mess (even if it gets cleared up later). It makes it impossible for the kids just to relax and enjoy themselves, in case they get grass stains on their trousers, or knock over the ketchup bottle.

I have another friend who is so obsessively competitive that his children are under huge pressure to win every friendly game they ever play. And one who frets excessively every time her child grazes his knees. I bet you can think of plenty of similar examples among people you know.

The really good parents I've encountered, on the other hand, expect their children to be noisy, messy, bouncy, squabbly, whingy and covered in mud. They take it all in their stride. They know they've got 18 years to turn these small creatures into respectable grown-ups, and they pace themselves. No rush to get them acting like adults – they'll get there in good time.

Between you and me, this Rule gets easier with time, though some people still never master it the way true Rules parents do. It's much harder to relax fully with your first baby than with your last teenager to leave home. With babies, you need to focus on the essentials – a healthy baby that isn't too hungry or too uncomfortable – and don't sweat the rest of it. It doesn't matter if their poppers are done up wrong, or you didn't find time to bath them today, or you've gone away for the weekend without anything for them to sleep in (yes, I have a friend who has done this, and no, she didn't sweat it, being a Rules parent).

Much better altogether if you can get to the end of each day, put your feet up with a glass of wine or a G&T,* and say cheerfully to each other, 'What the hell . . . they're all still alive so we must have got something right.'

> # REALLY GOOD PARENTS EXPECT THEIR CHILDREN TO BE NOISY, MESSY, BOUNCY, SQUABBLY, WHINGY AND COVERED IN MUD

---

* No, I'm not encouraging parents to use alcohol to get them through. Just relax!

Be yourself

Isn't it just so tempting to reinvent yourself when you meet somebody new who you really fancy? Or to try and be who you think they are looking for? You could become really sophisticated, or maybe strong and silent and mysterious. At least you could stop embarrassing yourself by making jokes at inappropriate moments, or being pathetic about coping with problems.

Actually, no you couldn't. At least, you might manage it for an evening or two, or even a month or two, but it's going to be tough keeping it up forever. And if you think this person is the one – you know, the one – then you might be spending the next half century or so with them. Just imagine, 50 years of pretending to be sophisticated, or suppressing your natural sense of humour.

That's not going to happen, is it? And would you really want a lifetime of lurking behind some sham personality you've created? Imagine how that would be, unable ever to let on that this wasn't really you at all, for fear of losing them. And suppose they find out in a few weeks' or months' or years' time, when you finally crack? They're not going to be very impressed, and nor would you be if it was them who turned out to have been acting out of character all along.

I'm not saying you shouldn't try to turn over the occasional new leaf; improve yourself a bit. We should all be doing that all the time, and not only in our love life. Sure, you can try to be a bit more organized, or less negative. Changing your behaviour is all fine and good. This Rule is about changing your basic personality. That won't work, and you'll tie yourself in knots trying to do it convincingly.

So be yourself. Might as well get it all out in the open now. And if that's not who they're looking for, at least you won't get in too deep before they find out. And you know what? Maybe they don't actually like sophisticated. Perhaps strong silent types don't do it for them. Maybe they'll love your upfront sense of humour. Perhaps they want to be with someone who needs a bit of looking after.

You see, if you fake it, you'll attract someone who belongs with a person that isn't you. And how will that help? Somewhere out there is someone who wants exactly the kind of person you are, complete with all the flaws and failings you come with. And I'll tell you something else – they won't even see them as flaws and failings. They'll see them as part of your unique charm. And they'll be right.

MIGHT AS WELL GET IT ALL OUT IN THE OPEN NOW

Printed in Great Britain
by Amazon